The Blazing Holy Fire

By Christine M Uwizera

PRESS

The Blazing Holy Fire

For speaking engagements, please contact:

The Blazing Holy Fire
P O Box 300552
Denver, CO 80203
USA
info@healingstream.net

Dedicated to:

Jesus My Redeemer: *Who once and for all saved me from the hands of satan and baptized me with the Holy Spirit and fire.*

&

My two siblings who have been subjects of (and answers to) my prayers for many years:

Assoumpta Kampundu: *Lost in the jungle during the war of Rwanda, kept and preserved by the Spirit of the Living God. She became an answer to our prayers 9 years later after she was found alive and well, washed by the blood of the Lamb. This was an answer to prayer.*

Jean Damascene Dirimasi: *Who since 1995 is a prisoner of war in Rwanda, at no fault of his own, but endures and trusts God to the very end.*

YOU ARE NEVER ALONE!

I found myself cast in the midst of fire but peace reigned within me. As I beheld His holy face, I was lifted far above my afflictions, oppression and terror. I looked down at the mountain of difficulties that were against me, but it was powerless to touch me! I said in my heart:

"Who is this God? Surely there has to be something different about Him!"
For the more I drew closer and sought Him earnestly,
the more opposition I met. Even though I was forced to give Him up,
I fell in love with Him instead... more and more!

In my trials I said: "No matter what I have to lose, I have to find Him, this Mighty God who prevails over all that has come against me and tried to stop me in my upward climb." I would in no way forsake my Savior - Jesus who took the punishment I deserved, and died the death on the cross to give me life! Oh, I would not give Him up! I chose the way of the cross. Since I refused to bow down and worship any other except God alone, the furnace was heated seven times hotter (Daniel 3:19). It was determined that I should be cast into the midst of a furnace of blazing fire where my enemies thought I would be finished, and where I would seek Him no more. *"Oh, the depth of the riches both of the wisdom and knowledge of God! How unsearchable are His judgments and unfathomable His ways"* (Romans 11:33)! It was in the midst of that fire that my soul found Him, the one I loved. What was meant to destroy me became instead a way to His heart. My soul clung to Him tightly, the one that I loved, and He upheld me with His right hand! Out of that fire, I saw His everlasting love and now I bring good tidings to you: "Be strong and let your heart take courage, all you who hope in the LORD" (Psalm 31:24).

Read on! You will hear the Holy Spirit speaking to you from the midst of the holy fire. You will be touched by God's consuming fire. You will catch the fire and become a dazzling pure flame that rises up through the igniting of the Holy Spirit's power, and you will bring joy, hope and warmth to every soul.

Great and incomparable are You
O God the Most High!
Glory and honor and power
Belong to you alone, Your Majesty on high!
How fortunate are those who trust in You
How blessed are those who draw near You
How blessed are those who dwell in Your presence
They are forever praising You!

Introduction

Y ou are holding more than a mere book in your hands. Behind these pages lies a message of fire with Christ's mighty power to permanently trans- form your lives. "Is not My Word like fire?" Declares the Lord, "and like a hammer which shatters a rock" (Jeremiah 23:29)? There will be an awakening in you as you read on. Those things that can be shaken, the worthless, the no-longer-good will be removed and that which cannot be shaken will remain and be strengthened.

At a time of fierce warfare, the message of God's holy fire was given to me. During such a great time of testing, I did not have anywhere to go or anyone to turn to except to Christ alone. I discovered that He is all that you need! In Him are found the revelations of all mysteries and answers to all of your problems. His comforting words and love beyond comprehen- sion came and saw me through it all. As time passed I fell in love with Him more and more. I was taken deeper into the depth of God's heart and now I invite you to join me in that journey.

Come nearer dear seeker, to God, the All Consuming Fire. Come closer and see. As you ascend to God, He will descend to you. You will hear the Holy Spirit speaking to you from the midst of the holy fire. You will be touched by God's consuming fire. You will catch the fire and become a dazzling pure flame that rises up by the igniting of the Holy Spirit's power bringing joy, hope and warmth to every soul and oh, child of God: change – change – change at any cost. Let yourself be kindled by the flame of fire for your Lord! You shall see, you shall know that this fire brings forth a light that permeates everything, everywhere and penetrates every darkness. The holy fire of God, it knows no boundaries, no limits and no failures!

The invitation is open for all. Neither education, nor experience, nor wealth, nor knowledge are needed to respond. God is in love with you already. God accepts you as you are, so come! Oh! Everyone who thirsts, come to the Fountain of Life and drink! To the thirsty, water will be given. They will drink and never be thirsty again. Let the frontline warriors, storm-tossed and afflicted, wounded in the battle-field, come to the Son of Righteousness in Whose wings you will find healing. Let them receive new strength! Oh, exhausted, feeble and anxious ones "Take courage, fear not." Sorrow and sighing must flee away in the presence of God's Holy Fire. Let all the seekers, far and near, draw closer. Seekers whether poor or rich, young or old, hurting or downcast, come! There is a place in God where all the burdens can be laid down and you will find rest and peace in Christ, the Prince of Peace.

If you read this book with an open heart, you will greatly benefit from the truths set forth behind these pages. I myself have turned to these pages and read this book many times; each time my life was deeply touched. It is my prayer that as God has blessed me with this message, so also that everyone who reads this book will be blessed and set on fire by the Holy Spirit.

Let your soul be swept away by the fire of holy passion. The old will burn. The wounds will be healed, leaving behind the splendor of Christ's life and His glory in you. You will be baptized in the Holy Spirit and fire! When this happens, no longer will you be a reader of the book of Acts, but you will live it daily. Yes, you will receive. You only need to believe, for all things are possible to him who believes. Remember, the gifts are of no use if not used! Once you are baptized in this fire, spread the fire to others; pass the fire on!

The bond servant,
Christine M Uwizera

Yours was a mission of redemption
O, blessed Lord Jesus!
Full of love and compassion,
You freely gave Your life for sinners and
You loved them to the very end!
As You said, "It is finished",
Salvation to all who come to You was accomplished.
Releasing them from their sins by Your blood,
They shall forever share the joy of heaven.
Oh the unfathomable Grace,
And Tender Mercies of our God,
Whose eyes are like a flame of fire!
Those who look upon You will be transformed,
Melted in the fire of Your love,
They will never be the same again.

Chapter 1: For Sinners Only!

God is seeking and searching for you. His arms are stretched out to you. Love and grace falling from His lips, Jesus lovingly addresses you: "Here am I, here am I." As He seeks you, would you let yourself be found? As He lovingly stretches His arms to embrace you, would you let yourself be loved?

> *"Listen, O heavens, and*
> *Hear, O earth;*
> *For the Lord speaks...*
> *An ox knows its owner*
> *And a donkey its master's manger*
> *But My people do not understand"*
> *(Isaiah 1:2, 3).*

"Oh, Divine Love, My God and My King! How do You look upon evil and still love? What do You feel as You look upon the children whom You created, loving and caring for them with undivided love, but alas Oh God many of them ignore You? They deny and reject You! All creation bows down at the sound

of Your name, but the man – the very one created in
Your own image – chooses to remain unmoved and
to reject You! Many deny You and go about their
business daily without giving You thought. Your
love towards them however still abounds! We see
Your sun shining on the sinners and the redeemed
alike; You send them rain in time of need. Great God,
Majestic in holiness: how infinite, how amazing, how
awesome, how vast is your love!"

Tell me, all you who hold this book in your hands:
what would happen to a new born baby if it rejects its
mother and father? Would there be any hope for life
for such a baby? Where is the hope of the ungodly?
The only hope they have is God! When they reject
Him, is there any hope left for them? The godless
are hopeless. Job saw their end and he lamented "For
what is the hope of the godless when he is cut off,
when God requires his life" (Job 27:8)?

There are many people who live in darkness. A
great and deep darkness! They come from all ranks
of life: poor or rich; learned or unlearned; religious
or not; low, medium or high class. When they have
lived in this darkness long enough, they become
unaware of it. Living carelessly in the habits of this
darkness, they are overtaken by the world and its
pleasures of sin that they are no longer able to see.
So in their inner most being, they experience fear and
doubts; like layers of thick mist, thus sinking deeper
and deeper into a void, into an emptiness. Isaiah
described them as people weighed down with iniquities. They negligently sit in darkness and they exist
under the shadow of death! To these God's great and

boundless love is coming towards them. He promises that "The people who were sitting in darkness saw a great light, and those who were sitting in the land and shadow of death, upon them a light dawned" (Matthew 3:16).

Be ready all you who have lived in darkness! There is a power from on high, a blazing holy fire that is coming your way, to destroy and consume all that has kept you in bondage for so long. This fire will cause chains to fall off from you. Iron doors will not prevail but will open by themselves. This fire will burn the old away, only the new will remain. Just believe, your Rescuer is coming to you. Be filled with expectation. Let hope arise in you, unimaginable possibilities are about to become a reality and you are about to be reborn and be a partaker in the kingdom of God. You shall then receive a new name.

Shake yourself from the dust. Rise up, oh captive ones. Those who said to you that there was no hope did not speak for God. Your God is a God of love and hope. Loose yourself from the chains around you. Be awake and clothe yourself in strength. Your Deliverer is right here. Look beyond the wars within and without, take courage and believe for He who comes to deliver you is mightier than any forces that have ever been. Let go of any voices of debating and reasoning. The reasoning of the wise is useless before God. Reason is of the earth and it can never reach heaven. It cannot grasp the spiritual things. When reason stops, faith begins and miracles take place. By His power, you will be pulled from the grave to the Light of His presence. There will be a new beginning for you. When this happens, take nothing of the old with you. You will experience a total disconnection from the old! Embrace your new life wholeheartedly. Believe! It is coming. A new beginning, a new journey!

Power of light over darkness

It is like a man who had stayed in the basement for a long time, and when he went outside, he was astonished to see the great light that was outside as it was during the summer and the sun was at its zenith. He enjoyed the new light and the enhanced sight even though it took him a while to get used to seeing such dazzling light. Upon returning in the basement, he was astonished at the darkness therein. He could barely see. He surely was able to see before encountering the greater light. Now he found that what was light before had become darkness! The real light had exposed darkness. What had been light could no longer be light because of the great light that surpasses it in glory. The light of God's presence is a powerful and true light, it will overcome any darkness. God is sending this light upon you and it will bring a revolution into your life. It is a greater light that will expose and chase darkness away. Time is expiring for all things that have stood in the way preventing you from truly seeing and advancing to your calling. The things that have kept you from living a full life are coming to an end! Time is running out for darkness because the light of God's presence has come.

There is therefore an enlightenment that takes place in each one's life when they encounter God, the All Light and the Almighty. This is the God you are about to encounter. He is the True Light that can enlighten every man. Of Him it was written "But as many as received Him, to them He gave the right to become children of God, even to those who believe in His name. Who were born, not of the blood nor of the flesh nor of the will of man but of God" (John 1:12-13).

Salvation is a free gift from God to you. You have been invited to receive this gift freely and willingly, for it will never be forced on anyone. Here is the key: to believe and receive. This free gift is Jesus Christ who came from heaven for you and for me to take away our sins. Use this key: believe Him and receive Him! In the same way the key will not be of any good if it is not used to open the door, the key you just received cannot be of any benefit without using it. You must act, so act. Believe Him and receive Him, and you will be saved. There is no other requirement to be saved; just believe and receive.

With the coming of the Light – the only one true light Jesus – darkness flees! The devil himself dwells in darkness and blinds people with darkness and causes them to sink deeper and deeper into an emptiness. He has no room where light is. He flees at the coming of the Light. He is only able to hide where he is hidden. Expose him by embracing the Light and he will at once run away from you! Darkness always flees at the coming of the light.

There is a revelation that takes place in the presence of the Light. Revelation means an enlightening or astonishing disclosure. You will be astonished at what you will discover in the Light of God's presence. What you do with revelation matters. What would you do if a thief were to be found in your house? If you would act in this situation which is temporary how much more do you need to act when you have a thief who wants to prevent you from spending endless of billions and trillions – innumerable happy years with God in heaven. This thief wants you to go to hell. I tell you, this is no small thief. Expel him from your property! Embrace the light. There is a great work that will be done in you when you come to the Light of God's presence. The Blazing Fire will help you, not only to get rid of the darkness in you, but you will help set others free who are living in the sea of darkness.

In the same way dust can hide in darkness behind the curtains but is exposed at the coming of the light and is at once removed; so will you let sin go. You must let it go in the name of Jesus "for the wages of sin is death but the free gift of God is eternal life in Christ Jesus our Lord" (Romans 6:23). Choose you today between sin and God's free gift of salvation. Choose wisely. Do not neglect to uproot sin from your life. Sin is a bad master for though many serve it, sin is not afraid to destroy their lives and it does so mercilessly. Come to Jesus, the Light of the world and you will be saved.

All things become new

You are about to be born again! You are about to receive a new name, which the mouth of the Lord will designate – all things will become new. Through God, everything will become different. Rejoice with me! Rejoice with heaven – what is about to take place is a great transformation for you!

Don't look back nor stand still.
Backward there is death,
Standing still is stagnation,
in other words death;
Going forward is Life – Eternal Life!

Come forward to the city of the Living God, come to the heavenly Jerusalem, come to the assembly of the redeemed and myriads upon myriads of angels. Come!

Oh, the greatness of God! Lift up your eyes and see who has created these stars! Leading them forth, God calls them all by name. The creator of the heavens and the earth and all their inhabitants is He. "By His word, the heavens were made and by the breath of His mouth all their host" (Psalm 33:6). He created the sea and the clouds. He placed boundaries on them all. "Thus far you shall come, but no farther," He spoke and it was done! He commanded and it stood fast. Who or what can you compare to His Majesty, God Almighty? The whole universe, all things and all people are held in existence by the might of His power. His sovereignty rules and reigns over all that is.

Bring the skilled wordsmith. Oh, let them create new words. Let them bring to birth a new language. For the language of mortals fails to describe the truth of the greatness of God! The story that one can share about Him in a lifetime can in no way paint in true colors His greatness. So come! Live it yourself! Once you discover this truth, you will surely join me and proclaim "O taste and see that the Lord is good" (Psalm 34:8.).

You who are proud in the thoughts of your hearts, with self-righteousness and good deeds reaching up to the sky, who told you that you can merit heaven by your own good deeds? Will you earn the uncreated with the created? God has made it clear in His word to you that flesh and blood cannot inherit the kingdom of God; nor does the perishable inherit the imperishable. Today God is extending this invitation to you also so that you might obtain your visa to heaven before you need to make that journey. Tomorrow waits for no one, let no one wait for tomorrow. Today is the day of your salvation. Only adulterous hearts turn away from following God, but you...accept Him today and start a new life. Jesus says: "Behold, I stand at the door and knock; if anyone hears My voice and opens the door, I will come in to him and will dine with him, and he with Me" (Revelation 3:20).

So open the door of your heart. Say "yes" to Jesus, let Him come in. Say a prayer from your heart but if you don't know how, pray with me:

*"Because of what Jesus has done for me, I come
to You, oh my heavenly Father. Forgive me for all
my sins. I repent. Today, I come back to You, oh
Source of Life. With my mouth I confess Jesus to be
my Lord and Savior. I receive the free gift of eternal
life through Jesus' death on the cross. I believe in
my heart that Jesus died for my sins and that by His
blood He paid the price for my salvation in full. I
believe that Jesus rose again from the dead and made
a way for me to be reunited with You. Oh, heavenly
Father, I renounce satan and I want to be yours. For
this I pray in the name of Jesus. Amen!"*

There is a great celebration at your new birth.
The angels, all the saints in heaven and on earth,
all things from everywhere are rejoicing. There is a
shout of joy in heaven and on earth because of your
spiritual birthday. Now, remember what God says
to you: "I have wiped out your transgressions like a
thick cloud. I have wiped out your sins like a heavy
mist. Return to me for I have redeemed you." (Isaiah
44:22).

Every sin you have ever committed has been
forgiven and forgotten by God who is the Great
Judge. You are a new creature. Believe that God sees
no stain on you. Let not the failures nor the sins of
the past haunt you because you have been forgiven
and you are now part of the saints and the family of
the Living God. Now "You are a chosen race, a royal
priesthood, a holy nation, a people for God's own
possession; so that you may proclaim the excellen-
cies of Him who has called you out of darkness into
His marvelous light" (1 Peter 2:9).

It is a new birth. Being born again is both the beginning of life and the end of death. Between this new life and the old life which was death, there is a string that connects life and death together. This string must be torn apart. There must be a total detachment from the old, from death. The Holy Spirit, the Spirit of the Living God will help you to tear it apart. Be open to receiving His guidance and heeding His voice.

You have set me on fire O Risen Savior,
You have touched me with Your consuming fire!
How my heart burns within me in response
to Your love!
You walk beside me,
You hold my hand.
Oh, how beautiful it is to be with You!
As You look into my eyes,
You see but Yourself in me.
As I look into my own eyes,
I see but You in me.
Deep into Your eyes
Mysteries of Your Word are revealed
You indeed have touched me with that
flaming sword!
Like the two on the road to Emmaus,
You have set my heart aflame
You have unveiled my eyes
And Oh, I will recognize You anew every day!

Chapter 2: Infinite Perpetual Heavenly Fire

Five fingers on one hand, behold there are four gaps between them! Five mountain tops, between them four valleys! Being on the mountain tops only five times means there were four times when you were in the valley, in the gap. If you are on fire for God only on Sundays, this means there are six days a week when you live without the fire! What happens during those six days when the fire is out? Danger! Even if one were to be on fire for God six days a week, beware! "Do not put out the Spirit's fire" ᴺᴵⱽ (1 Thessalonians 5:19), because wherever fire is out, there is no light. Being on fire often, or numerous times, or even several times is not good enough either. Often, many times etc… these are all small pieces, portions that don't last; they cannot satisfy one in whose heart God has already placed eternity (Ecclesiastes 3:11). They cannot help you to have a heavenly fire which is whole and eternal. It is an infinite, continual heavenly fire that never goes out.

The Holy Spirit is calling you to catch this infinite perpetual fire and to keep it always burning.

"Keep your light lit," our Lord said! Each child of God must therefore keep the lamp lit and be always dressed in readiness. It was the virgins whose lamps went out that missed the wedding feast. The virgins whose lamps were lit entered in with the bridegroom for they were always ready. When you are always ready, you can be used by God at any time, anywhere. If you are ready you are useful. If you are not ready, you are useless. Be always ready, oh bride of Christ. In season and out of season, remain ready. It is not only for pastors, teachers and those who oversee the ministry to be ready, but it is the task of every believer to always keep the lamp lit. "Only the light of the ungodly goes out, and their flame gives no light" (Job 18:5).

John the Baptist said that when Jesus comes "He will baptize you with the Holy Spirit and fire" (Matthew 3:11). This fire referred to by John the Baptist was a heavenly fire. That's why He Who comes from above was the only One Who could baptize people in such fire because it was a fire from above.

The baptisms of water and of fire are both important. Unlike the water baptism however, the baptism of fire is not performed by any human agent but by Jesus through the Holy Spirit. It is heavenly fire. It is a perpetual fire, a constantly burning inward fire that never goes out! When believers catch this constant fire, they no longer know momentary heights, nor do they descend to lower altitudes, nor achieve sporadic mountain tops, but they experience daily heights and mountain tops in the spiritual realm. God is calling His bride to be always at the highest peak – at the mountain top – for there the glory of the Lord dwells. That's where the consuming fire abides. To be always at the highest peak requires a continuous, constant fire burning in the believer's heart, a never-ending holy inward flame. "Fire shall be kept burning continually on the altar; it is not to go out" (Leviticus 6:13).

Fire for forerunners

There is a tremendous need to prepare the way of the Lord, saving the lost and snatching them out of the fire before it is too late. As you look around, you see a great number of people who live as though this world is all there is. This world is their home. However, those who have no home in heaven are actually homeless! You don't have to go too far to see these lost souls. Look around where you live, where you work, your church, and your school. Look and alas, you will find many who neglect the Lord! Oh how terrible will be the day when their lives on earth are finished and they have to stand before God to give account of what they did for Jesus and the salvation He secured for them. Now they walk around trusting in their own good deeds, thinking of themselves as more upright than God Himself and even though they were offered an opportunity to receive Him, they refused. They do not ask, they do not seek, they do not knock; for if they did they would find and if they knocked, the door would be opened for them. They may seem to do good, however there is a day coming when their own righteousness will be exposed for what it is: sinfulness. Their own good deeds and self righteousness will be turned into filthy rags and the things of this world they invested in will flee from them saying "I could help there, but I cannot help here!" Silver and gold will not be able to deliver them in the day of Judgment. "And in those days men will seek death and will not find it; they will long to die, and death flees from them" (Revelation 7:6).

Bride of Christ, see what is about to befall them and may the forerunner come to their rescue before it is too late! Who is going to confront these people and turn them to the Lord their God except He who is ready to preach the message of John the Baptist, even the message of Jesus Christ, for we see both giving the same message: "Repent for the kingdom of God is at hand" (Matthew 3:2; 4:17). When John preached this message, he had this constant burning fire and that's why multitudes felt the conviction of their sins and came asking him *"What should we do?"* Oh, saints of the Living God, when you are fired up like John the Baptist, you will see many running to you asking *"What should we do?"* John the Baptist was a forerunner, the one who came before Christ in the Spirit and power of Elijah. He made ready a people prepared and ready for the Lord. He was a burning and shining light and he prepared the way of the Lord. He was always ready, in season and out of season.

John the Baptist ran the race; he did his task very well and finished it very strongly. Today however, there are many who are still sitting in darkness. God is sending light into this darkness, and He will send more through you. It is your task to be a burning light. How can you burn if you have not caught the fire yet? Have you received this fire? Are you keeping it or do you just have it once in a while and then it goes out again till the next revival meeting? Wake up! Be baptized in the fire so that you will be full of fire and keep it constantly. Be stirred up. "Be broken, O peoples and be shattered" (Isaiah 7:9). When you are shaken, fear not. It is in being shaken that you bring forth fruits! A tree full of apples is shaken because fruits are expected of it. If there is a shaking in you, it is because something is expected of you. So be shaken and bring forth fruits.

Oh, let me tell you about the shaking that takes place and separates the worthy grain from the worthless! Only the wheat grains that have been harvested from the field and have been tossed are allowed to go into a sieve where they would then be shaken. So at first the worthy and the unworthy grain are threshed together in a sieve. The farmer shakes the sieve vigorously until the remaining weeds, dust, and chaff, the-no-longer beneficial rise. There they are collected together on one side and are thrown on the heap of refuse where they are cast away. The worthless grain and straw are completely removed while the good grain which is whole is chosen. Chaff and straw must be cast away but never the worthy grain. When God allows a shaking in believers' lives, it is to their benefit. In the same way straw has nothing in common with grain, and so they must be separated.

God's shaking in the life of a believer brings separation, removing the chaff, the dead from that which is of the kingdom of God. Like the shaking of the grain in the sieve, the heavenly fire of God will shake those who receive it. This shaking purifies and refines them until they become whole, and finally they become forerunners who will make ready a people prepared for the Lord.

A supernatural baptism

"He will baptize you with the Holy Spirit and fire" (Matthew 3:11).

The baptism of the Holy Spirit and fire is a supernatural baptism performed not by the hand of man but by Jesus through the Holy Spirit upon a believer. He who comes from above is above all. This baptism is from above and it is for all the children of God who desire a deep walk with God and want to be of the mountain top, of above. It is after this baptism that you will effectively and fully do the work of God, walking in signs and wonders. It is marvelous to live and move in the supernatural. The kingdom of God does not consist in words but in power. The Gospel of Jesus Christ is the power of God. When it is preached, there must be a demonstration of power. Paul's message and preaching were not in persuasive words of wisdom, but in demonstration of the Spirit and supernatural power from heaven (1 Corinthians 2:4).

When the Gospel is preached and is not however demonstrated with signs and wonders following and confirming the Word, something is wrong; something is being stolen from the true Gospel and it is as if the Gospel itself is taken to the cemetery where it is laid in the grave! A memorial! People will visit this memorial, they will learn some truths about it, but it's not living! The authentic word of God however is preached with power and it will not be buried but will go deep into the hearts of men, causing a resurrection to take place in the lives of those who hear it. The true Gospel will be preached with power, being confirmed by signs and wonders.

How many today have buried the Word of God in the grave, in the tomb? How many? Oh, merciful God, help and rescue the people called by Your Name. Unveil the eyes of all so that none would lay Your Word in the tomb. You who have buried the Truth in the tomb, it is time to roll the stone away. It is time to let that stone fall away and let the Living Word out. It is time to let go of religion and theology and the habit. It is time to embrace the new. Your word, oh God, is too beautiful to be buried. Your word is powerful and mighty! Your word is the power unto salvation, salvation from the power of sin, salvation from all bondages, salvation from sickness and diseases, salvation from all oppressions. Your Word, oh God, is a flaming sword, a two-edged sword that is living, active and quick to perform and fulfill all of Your promises and desires.

Jesus commanded the disciples to wait for this baptism of the Holy Spirit and fire. Even though they had been called of God, they were not fully released to do the ministry with signs and wonders in such a great way until they received power from on high, on the day of Pentecost. Before this baptism, they were just good disciples but they were still full of flesh and that's why many times they forsook Him and fled; that's why they denied Him and some betrayed Him. But see what took place after they received the baptism of the Holy Spirit and fire: they made God's power known. No longer did they deny Him but they died for Him! No longer did they doubt Him but they believed in Him.

Child of God, you need to be baptized with the Holy Spirit and with fire. You ought to be clothed with power from on high. Being baptized with the Holy Spirit and fire means to be immersed into the fullness of God's holy fire to the extent that you become a light to the world (Matthew 5:14) and a flame of fire (Psalm 104:4).

The fire and the believer

God wants to make His power known to everyone using you and me. This is a supernatural power that will not flow through flesh and carnal vessels because these will only be reduced to ashes instead of transmitting God's power. Any vessel that is purified by God's cleansing fire will be a true channel through which this supernatural power of God will flow and touch other people's lives.

Today we have many ministers but only a handful of them are walking in God's power as it was in the first church. The reason is because many have not received the baptism of the Holy Spirit and fire or they have lost the fire by not keeping it lit; therefore they can preach good sermons about the Holy Bible's precepts but they are unable to demonstrate what they preach. Miracles are being taught but never seen, so those whose faith is weak run to seek in other places. The lack of power in churches is causing many to run to psychics and New Age doctrines and the name of the Lord is being blasphemed all because of those who are called by the name of the Lord yet are not walking in His power!

Oh, let those who are called by the name of the Lord draw nearer to Him, let them leave behind excuses and believe. Let them believe that the fire of God is for all and that it is about to come upon those who wait and diligently seek the Lord.

There are those who want to receive but they are afraid of the fire of God – that river of fire that flows and comes out from before God Almighty, whose throne is ablaze while its wheels are burning with fire (Daniel 7:9-10). Be not afraid you child of the Most High. Be not like those who said "Let me not hear again the voice of the Lord my God, let me not see this great fire anymore, or I will die" (Deuteronomy 18:16). God has not given you a spirit of fear but of power, of love and of a sound mind. Have the mind of Christ and you will have a sound mind and not have the fear of fire. Let the devil alone be afraid of the fire and hate it, but let the children of God receive and embrace this Holy Fire and love it.

There are others who believe that this fire is only for the new born experience. To these, God is calling them to go back to the first love, which they have lost.

Others believe that it was only for those disciples in the book of Acts. Those believers forget that they are also called to be disciples of Jesus Christ, for He said, "Go therefore and make disciples of all the nations" (Matthew 28:19). You and I are the disciples. Remember that all Jesus' disciples throughout the ages are commanded to observe all things Christ asked of the early disciples. Jesus is the same, yesterday, today and forever (Hebrews 13:8).

Others believe in this fire because they used to have the fire but now it is gone. They went through many trials, many problems in their lives and the fire died because it was a weak fire! To these God wants them to know that there is a holy strong blazing heavenly fire that can never be put out by the wind. Only a feeble fire needs protection from the wind. The fire from on high is powerful. The wind and the storm are not able to put the heavenly fire out. This is the fire God is about to release in you, if you are willing. All things are possible to those who believe. So be willing, desire the fire but don't stop there. To will is not a step forward. Act. Yes, there must be an act from you; faith without works is dead! So act. Remember that staying with your old way of doing things, the habits, is routine. Stepping out to embrace the new is acting!

Have you found yourself on the mountain top many times and then in the valley many times? Up and down, back and forth, around and around the mountain thus never advancing...away with this routine. Believe and be on fire for Jesus, you casual Christian! People who are neither hot nor cold will be spit out His mouth. Burn with a heavenly fire. It is an eternal fire; keep it always, forever and a day. Never live a second without it, never let it go, it is yours. Come, infinite and perpetual fire!

My soul panted and thirsted for the Lord,
Him alone I desired.
Above life itself I wanted God,
Him alone I sought earnestly!
"Where are You My God?" I cried,
God heard and answered from on high.
The Holy Spirit came and took me by the hand,
He led me through the mountain of fire,
There the journey to catch the fire began!

Chapter 3: Catching the Heavenly Fire

"Keep the fire! The fresh fire you received when you first believed!" David Hocker, a young godly man who carried the fire of God since He was fourteen years old warned me of the danger if my first love and fresh fire for God were lost. I was in a prayer meeting and I had just shared in very few words about a burning experience I had when I first came to know the Lord. Many at the church and in that group were touched by this testimony but when young David heard that the fresh fire was not in me as it used to be, he was filled with boldness and confronted me. He begged me to be in that place where the fire always burns. He told me that it was a great danger if I chose to be outside the fire and made only sporadic visits to the fire once in a while. Like a man awakened from sleep, I was shaken and touched to the core. Was it possible to gain back and keep the fresh fire I felt during the first weeks of my salvation? Oh, those weeks – it was a great honeymoon with the Lord! If it was possible to have this fresh fire again, I wanted it at any cost.

How I thank God for this rebuke. It awoke me and it revolutionized my walk with Christ ever since! You see, from day number one when I gave my life to Jesus Christ, I only wanted His fullness and nothing less. Along the way however, without me even realizing it, I lost the burning fire. The words spoken to me by this young man in this meeting in early 2002 would not leave me for several weeks. They echoed through my entire being for a long time "Keep the fire! The fresh fire you received when you first believed!"

My quest started here with a determination to arouse myself, seek God and get hold of Him. To seek God above all things; not the fire, nor the gift, nor the reward, nor the created, but the Creator. Christ is the one who baptizes with the Holy Spirit and fire. He who truly finds God also finds the fire because God lives in the midst of the fire (Ezekiel 1).

The quest

With this quest, a great journey began! Amazingly, to this day the journey continues! And great things have happened along the way. I was astonished that the more I seek God the more I want Him. The more thirsty and hungry I become, the more I seek, and the more I want Him. Indeed, he who goes all-out towards God never wearies. I sought Him whom my soul loves so. There is a price to pay and it has to be paid daily. Seeking God and gaining back the fire costs me all things. I lost my honor, titles, some family members, and many people I believed were friends and eventually I lost all of those things. I gained far more than I lost, however. It is in losing all that I fully found Christ, who is all to me.

I'm now speaking to the seeker: "No matter what you are seeking, you will find it." "Let not your heart faint because of the time. It is not for you to know times or epochs which the Father has fixed by His own authority" (Acts 1:7-8). Seek without looking at the time. Seek and you will find. To the thirsty, He will give water. To the hungry, He will provide bread. So here is wisdom: Thirst after Divine drink only. Divine drink alone quenches your thirst. If you thirst after the drink of this world, you will find it (fame, immorality, drinking, worldly power, recognition and more of this world), but it only destroys because it is a cursed cup containing a bitter drink. Seeker – thirst and hunger only after God! Seek what is only Life for no matter what you are seeking you will find it! Either life or death! Seek with wisdom!

So I sought God earnestly with all my heart. Day and night I sought Him through prayer and soaking in God's presence. I also fasted and spent all my free time with the Lord. I found His love to be better than anything. As I drew closer to Him, He drew closer to me. I was drawn to Him so deeply that I would fall on my knees each time I got an opportunity and talk with Him like to a friend. I read His Word and worshipped Him constantly and I fell in love more and more every single day.

Whether it took a long time or not, I do not know. Somehow, time was not an issue for me; I came to be baptized in the fire. A Holy Fire, which was an inner burning force that came from the Father of Light, an unusual and consuming fire. When this fiery baptism took place in my life, the Spirit of the Lord and His fire came mightily upon me from that day forward and have not left me ever since. I love this fire and to me life has no meaning if I am not on fire for Jesus. This fire is so great and powerful that it has changed me and left all the people around me changed! It is such a mighty fire that is exceedingly so great, and so uncontrollable that it has set ablaze all that come in contact with me. All sinners that have been in my company have come to know the Lord without me begging them to change! This fire is so violent that it invaded and took over without asking permission. This fire cannot be held by anyone or anything. When a believer is given this baptism of fire, it cannot be contained in them. Rather it spreads and touches all that come closer to the one who carries it. Oh, yes, this fire has no measure. You can take as much as you are able to handle and then you can pass it on. The fire of God has no limits, only one's capacity to pass it on can be limited and that is the only way people can limit this fire in their lives.

It thus invaded all, even sinners who sat with me at work were changed within hours and they would be filled with the fullness of God. Many of them would receive Christ and radiate His glory and be filled with the Holy Spirit at the same time – I can remember when one stood up in front of a multitude of unbelievers at work and confessed: "I think I caught an addiction and that is God. I must confess I am in love with Jesus." Some will be filled with holy laughter, something they had never seen or heard of before. In most cases I do not have to force open doors, but if necessary I would! The fiery presence of this fire, so heavy and mighty causes the captives to see the light and see how they were on their way to hell and they come to accept Christ without resistance. Each time one receives salvation, the Lord allows me to live the new-born experience again and joy floods my soul. At those times I feel as though I am living in heaven even though I go through the most trying hard times of my life.

We must have this fire. We must be the dweller of the light brought by this blazing holy fire! Awake you who are called by the Name of the Lord. If you are not affecting or changing sinners and lives around you, it is probably because you are living conformed to this world. If the presence of God is strong in you, you must see sinners changed. And if you are not changing them, they are unknowingly changing you. If you say they are not changing you, how sad it will be for you to go to heaven alone, seeing your own brothers and sisters and friends in the lake of fire! The time is very short for His second coming and we must save them from the torment of hell. At any cost let's take them all with us to heaven! Let's shame the devil and empty the pits of hell he has prepared for these.

God's table is always prepared for the one who is hungry. His cup is always filled for them that are thirsty. Become a seeker, a very thirsty and hungry one, and the Lord will prove Himself faithful in providing you with His drink and His bread. When you diligently seek the Lord then He will let you find Him and the nearer you will get to God, the greater the intensity of the fire you will receive. God is an all-consuming fire. If you want to keep warm, you must come closer and closer to the fire. If you want more of God's holy fire, you must come closer to God. So, draw closer to God and you will encounter God, the All Consuming Fire. And remember that this is the same All Powerful God who sent the violent rushing wind and the tongues of fire upon those disciples who were in the upper room.

The calling

In 1998, the Lord called me through the mouth of a prophet in Seattle, WA. By then I was a new Christian and when I received God's calling I trembled. I was hit by the words I heard from the heart of God: "I have set you apart to serve me." "How could that be?" I wondered. In earthly terms, I was less likely to be chosen not only by God but by even any other person! Who was that one that would desire to choose me? I come from Rwanda, a very small country, about the size of the state of Maryland. This country was the poorest at the time of this calling, and it was known mostly by the killings that took place in 1994 where close to one million people killed each other within three months. At one time, this country and its people were despised and insignificant to most of the world. We used to be embarrassed when people would ask what country we were from! That country whose citizen killed one another, that country which drank the blood of many innocent lives! My life was doubly wounded during this perilous time because I lost three siblings, many other family members and numerous friends. How could it be that God would choose such a one as I? Though I went through that hard time, I had received total healing in 1997, which was the day when I accepted the Lord Jesus Christ into my life.

Besides coming from that small country, I saw myself as just an insignificant person and these words from a prophet seemed too good to be true. I believed them, however. The Holy Spirit reminded me that when Jesus came to this earth, those who were in palaces and considered themselves to be learned did not recognize Him as the Savior. Instead, they missed the time of their visitation. We see King Herod among them "Now Herod was very glad when he saw Jesus, for he had wanted to see Him for a longtime" (Luke 23:8). Why did not Herod see Jesus any time He wanted to? He had all the power in the whole world to see Him any time, anywhere, anyhow but he did not. However, in the Bible we see the fishermen, the outcasts, the sinners, the humble, the brokenhearted and the despised reclining at the table with Jesus and sitting at His feet! How true it is that "God has chosen the weak things of the world to shame the things which are strong, and the base things of the world and the despised God has chosen, the things that are not so that He may nullify the things that are" (1 Corinthians 1:27-28).

When I received this calling I prayed to God and asked Him to equip and anoint me for His work. I also sought God earnestly. I requested Him to confirm this calling by ordaining me. The invitation to be ordained came 5 years after I heard God calling me, 5 years after praying for this calling day and night. This invitation came from God Himself because I never requested to be ordained from anyone, I trusted God that if He truly chose me He would have to ordain me along the way somehow. Dear saints, though you might doubt the calling of God upon your life, God does not doubt it. Though you might forget your prayers due to waiting for so long, God never forgets your prayers. Hold on to every word God spoke to you. God is watching over His word to perform it (Jeremiah 1:12). I was quite shocked and I trembled at the reality of knowing how God is faithful to His words and promises. Dear saints, be encouraged! Fear not; His promises will all come to pass.

Apostle Paul Gitwaza

Paul Gitwaza, known in Rwanda as the Apostle Paul, is a friend of God and a yielded vessel that God is using in a mighty revival that is sweeping through the nation of Rwanda. God has used this man to bring the heavenly fire into many people's hearts in different nations. Apostle Paul preaches the Gospel with such authority and power from on high that signs and wonders are natural in his meetings.

I had met Paul Gitwaza during the first month of my conversion in Kigali, Rwanda in 1997. Oh, how beautiful was the body of Christ in the gathering of "Inkuru Nziza" meaning "Good News" where I first believed and was saved! It was there I truly came to know the Holy Scripture in action without reading it! In this place, Christians would meet daily at noon and worship God. Shepherds and sheep would come to the throne of God in one accord. They would set aside their denominations and their own agendas, come in one mind continually devoting themselves to seeking God. This they would do from Monday through Friday. On Saturday and Sunday, they would have fellowship in their own congregations. In this congregation, I saw the power of God in action to such a degree that when I first read the Holy Word, I read what I had already seen with my own eyes!

By that time Apostle Paul was a young man in his twenties. The first time I saw him he was invited to pray and close the fellowship at Inkuru Nziza. As he started praying, there was such an outpouring of God's Spirit and power. I could feel bolts of fire coming forth as the words crossed his mouth. Miracles of all sorts took place throughout the entire building. The Spirit of the Lord came mightily upon Paul and revelations of the things to come came through his mouth. To me he said that in three days the Lord was pleased to bless me with a job. I had been jobless for six months and I had not told anyone in that gathering about my situation. Though I was a babe in Christ, I believed this word to be true and of God. I never questioned it. It was a Friday around 1:30 p.m. when I received this word. Monday about the same time, I had missed the gathering because a dear friend whom I wanted to reach for the Lord had requested me to train her in how to use a computer. While we were just starting, a man who had an important position in the United Nations walked in and offered me a position to run his office and to help with his computer work. I got the job without an interview and without looking for it – Praise God! The job came looking for me and the word of God through the mouth of Apostle Paul Gitwaza came to pass. Though Paul didn't know me at that time, I knew beyond a shadow of a doubt that our paths would cross again. It would happen years later through a divine appointment and it would be at that moment when an endless burning fire descended upon me in a mighty way, radically changing me and all those who have ever come to be in contact with me!

Ablaze with flames of fire

Then it came: a tangible, perpetual, powerful fire ignited in me by the power of the Holy Spirit. It was a fire of God's burning holiness, a fire of God's fiery love. "He will baptize you with the Holy Spirit and fire" (Luke 3:16).

It was on the day of Pentecost when I was baptized in this blazing holy fire from heaven. It was a baptism of fire that burns away the chaff and everything that cannot pass through the fire. It was a kind of fire that I had never known before. It was the kind of fire that never goes out because God Himself is its source. This fire is all consuming, and was a new force that would soon help me to effectively do the work of God.

It was during the month of May and that day a dear sister in the Lord, Sherry Collins who had traveled with me reminded me it was Pentecost. I had forgotten that this day was Pentecost, and once I realized it, I was drawn into God's presence. That day I was ordained by Apostle Paul Gitwaza and what a great present my heavenly Father sent down to me! It was a great surprise because before this I did not know nor understand the baptism of fire. Father, You gave me without measure – more than I could think or imagine. O, Righteous One, You indeed know the longing and yearning of our hearts. There is nothing good that You withhold from those who love You and earnestly seek You. Drawn into Your presence, my God and my King, Your Spirit came over me and rested upon me. I awoke engulfed in the blaze of Your holy flames. It was a new flame, the never-known before, the never-experienced before.

Several months before this baptism, I had been seeking God passionately. During this time of seeking God there was born in me a great yearning and longing to know God and to be with Him always. As I kept seeking, there seemed to be a great expectation of something that was about to take place in my life, but I did not know what it was. I then received a word from my spiritual father, Apostle Paul Gitwaza of Zion Temple in Rwanda, that He was coming to conduct a revival meeting in the USA and that the Lord laid it on his heart to ordain me! He requested that I consecrate myself and be ready for this great day.

The ordination took place in Dayton, OH on a Memorial Day weekend of 2004. The Spirit of God moved mightily in this three-day revival meeting, which started as early as ten in the morning and lasted until between ten and midnight! A great number of people were touched by the power of God in those meetings right in their seats without anyone laying hands on them. Many more would still be touched by the power of God when back in their dorms and in their cars even after the meeting was finished. The presence of God from that first day was heavy and it got thicker and thicker by the hour. I started getting by myself and soon the things of this world drew further and further away and I found myself drawn closer and closer to God. What used to be important and dear to me seemed not to be important any more – how could this be? What I valued most, I came to value least!

When we would arrive at our dorms after the meetings, I had no desire to sleep. How could this be? After giving my life to Christ, I had told Him I would give up anything but I had said "You know how much I enjoy sleeping in and taking naps, please dear Lord don't take this away from me. I will give up anything, but leave me to sleep as much as I want." This time however, I had no desire to go to sleep. Rather, I wanted to be with the Lord. I could not stop thinking about Jesus. After we arrived at the dorms, I would watch into the night with the Lord and some-times minister to my dear brothers and sisters who had come to the meetings. Appetite for food disap-peared and in its place a divine appetite arose within me and within many people's hearts who attended those meetings. I could only sleep two to three hours a night. I was in such a great deep love with my Adonai that I could not help but think about Him the whole time. It was like falling in love with the prince of my dreams; I was barely able to sleep.

The second day of the revival was incredible. The worship of Voice Ministries of IHOP (International House of Prayer) from Michiana lead by Bob Deering only increased the presence of God in the meetings. These singers were so anointed and sang propheti-cally and they brought the presence of God down to us. I have visited their 24x7 house of worship and prayer and had seen that God's presence is very real in this ministry. That day, as they sang, there began a great shaking and trembling that took place within me and without. I was to be ordained in a couple hours and I could barely contain the joy of the Lord I felt!

Very soon, it was time for a break but worship was non-stop. We went for lunch which was to take place in the same room where we held our meetings. There the beautiful worship by Voice Ministries IHOP Michiana was ongoing. I was sitting at the table and across the table from me was a young man, Gustave, who held his fork in his hands unable to eat simply because God's presence was heavy in the house. We all could not eat! We left our full plates and quickly found corners and got on our knees. Oh, the presence of God; how awesome and how magnificent! There in that corner, I made my wedding vow to God:

My Adonai
Today, receive my wedding vow to You
I give You me
I vow to be Yours and only Yours
I vow to die with You my Jesus, to live through You
and only for You
I vow that I will love You
With all my heart
With all my soul
With all my strength

I was lost into God's presence. There I sensed the heat hovering all over and around me like a hot wind. The Holy Spirit's presence was heavy in that place. Very soon, the meetings resumed. When my name was called, I stood together with my brothers and sisters in the Lord who were also ordained. Very soon, hands were laid upon me by Apostle Paul Gitwaza and he told me "Christine, God does not lie. What He promised to you has been fulfilled today."

A dozen pastors who had come with Apostle Paul joined and prayed for all of us by the laying on of hands. That heat indeed was the Pentecostal fire, for I saw tongues of fire coming and resting upon many of us. God's Holy Fire came upon me at that moment in an unusual way. The burning started in me and then it was as if I could hear the Holy Spirit speaking to me: "Away with the old! You could not wear a new garment without taking off the old one!"

This fire indeed burned and its flames touched me! The old in me was burned away. As all the old things burned away, I became aware that this was a heavenly Pentecostal fire that I had desired for so long. Ablaze with flames, I trembled and shook within and without.

The Pentecostal fire

I received this fire. It was the fire of Pentecost. This fire seemed to be coming from within me and then outward! At times it would go through my entire being and then it seemed to penetrate everywhere I was: on the ground, on people and on things around me and then again within me and through me. At times, it would be like the rain of fire coming from everywhere. It was a stream of fire, streaming inward and outward. To this day, this fire races back and forth. I shook and I trembled. This was only the second day of revival; the third day would be even more powerful, for the fire increased its intensity every single moment.

I could feel the heat and it followed wherever I went. At times, it would feel as though I was clothed in a cloak of fire and light. The appetite for food and sleep was gone for a while. We would spend the nights praising God and rejoicing for all that He was doing. The sinners who came to those meetings believed God and gave their lives to the Lord. Those who at first thought we were crazy for dancing in those meetings were the first people to be saved. We saw the backslidden repent and we saw true reconciliation between the two tribes of Rwanda and Burundi. Because of political wars and killings in those nations, these two tribes came to hate one another but during this revival meetings, they stepped forward and confessed their sins to one another. Forgiveness took place and the joy of the Lord filled all of us. I remember that on the last day, when I finally got my appetite back, I went to McDonalds to eat. But I was not able to talk in English; I was speaking in other tongues. It took me quite a while before I would be able to order food, I was filled with holy laughter and I did not know how to stop it. I was so drunk with the Holy Spirit that instead of ordering food, I told people about the Lord.

This fire continued and for many weeks, I would shake and tremble. During the time of worship, prayer, fellowship, or just thinking about my Savior Jesus, the intensity of this fire would increase. Many times, I would feel myself vibrating as though I had a consuming fire within. Five days after this baptism, I could still see the cloak of light on me and the intensity of the fire. I was excited by this fire but one day when I woke up, I had a visitation of "doubts": "What if this fire ceases after all? What if it was just for that moment because I was in revival?" I doubted. As I started doubting, I found that I had lost my freedom by allowing the voice of the evil one to speak to me. For a short time I did not feel the power of this fire racing through me as it usually does. I started crying out to God and as I went to bed that night, I woke up with much fire on me and I heard the voice of the Holy Spirit telling me: "I will never desert you, nor will I ever forsake you" (Hebrews 13:6). Ever since that time, I have been given the grace to have this perpetual fire non-stop and I don't want to live one day without it. Since I received this baptism, from glory to glory and from power to power I must go. When you receive the baptism of fire you will not lose it because He who baptizes you is faithful. This fire is eternal; it cannot be taken away from you unless you choose to. One can choose to leave God but as long as you walk with God and you are His, He will never leave you nor forsake you.

Pentecostal fire for all

"And there appeared to them tongues as of fire distributing themselves, and they rested on each one of them. And they were all filled with the Holy Spirit and began to speak with other tongues, as the Spirit was giving them utterance" (Acts 2:3-4).

The first baptism of the Holy Spirit and fire recorded in the Bible took place on the day of Pentecost. Tongues of fire fell upon all 120 believers who were in the upper room. None was left out without being touched by tongues of fire; none was left out without being touched by the Holy Spirit. United that day in the upper room, the disciples saw a violent rushing wind descending from heaven filling them all with the Holy Spirit and fire, and the promise of God was thus fulfilled (Matthew 3:11). Jesus who baptizes in the Holy Spirit and fire has never changed. He is the same yesterday, today and forever. If it happened then, it must still happen today. The Holy fire is available for all Jesus' disciples throughout the ages. But alas; today many people don't even know that there is something such as God's holy fire. Also only a few believe in it and desire it. It is time to have the baptism of fire restored back to the body of Christ.

This baptism of the Holy Spirit and the fire did not take place before Jesus' ascension to heaven, for He had said "for if I do not go away, the Helper will not come to you, but if I go, I will send Him to you" (John 16:7). Jesus had to be glorified first and then the fire would come after His glorification. People in the Old Testament have an excuse for not having this baptism of fire, but now there remains no more excuses. Jesus is faithful, He went and just as He promised He sent the Holy Spirit. The Holy Spirit is here today among God's people. He is moving among the believers but only a few recognize Him and His ministry of fire. A handful accepts His ministry. If today's church chooses to close the doors on Him, how can they then have power, for it is written "You will receive power when the Holy Spirit has come upon you" (Acts 1:8). If He does not come upon you, you are but a powerless and weak vessel. But praise God that you have Him.

In my imagination I can see the fire falling and resting upon the 120 people in the New Testament church and the tongues of fire coming and resting on each one! The rushing wind filling the whole place! I don't see any who were left out. Let no one have an excuse that pastor so and so got all of it because he is much anointed and that there is not enough left. Oh, no, no, no! The Bible tells us that the tongues of fire distributed themselves and rested upon each individual. These tongues did not rest only on Apostle John, who was Jesus' best friend, nor on James, nor on Peter only. They distributed on each of the 120 in the upper room. Even Thomas got it! There is enough fire for you and for everyone who is willing and has faith. Even if 99% of all the people on the entire planet would receive this baptism of fire, there would still be more than enough for you, more than you can contain. The wells of the Holy Spirit are always full and the storeroom of heaven can never run out. God Himself, source of all sources, is the Source of this fire. In the kingdom of God there is no lack but abundance. There will be plenty forever and ever more.

Don't be afraid to pass this fire on because you think you will not have enough for yourself. No, no, no my brothers and sisters. This fire is not given to you to hold. In fact it is only given to those who will pass it on. Even though this fire is powerful and of such a great benefit it can also harm those who try to hold it for themselves grudgingly. This fire is so strong that if you try to hold it you will only be harming yourself. Too much fire held by one person would be like a scorching heat that causes sunburn. Sunburn is but an excess of heat and it only harms. Too much fire held by one person can become like a fever caused by disease, an excess of heat in a body. As you know, fever is not good for the body.

Pass on the fire! If you hold it, you will lose it. Be not like those who are afraid to lend their spiritual books to their friends for fear that the receiver will be more fired up for the Lord and have more power than the giver. Jealousy has no room in the kingdom of our God and it must be uprooted from the body of Christ. Jealousy and competition must not be among the fire carriers. Share about this baptism of fire, experience and teach about this fire to everyone. Wherever you go, start the fire. Wanting to be the only person with the gift and the power is not good and God would not want to be a part of that power. Freely you have received, now freely give. Let the motive of your heart be always pure. Share all you have with everyone, see the miracle of multiplication. Pass it on. Pass it on. Pass it on, my friend! You will find out that the fire you give out will come back to you only multiplied. This fire is so strong that many times when I have been at home seeking the Lord or if I have been in the heavy presence of the Lord, I have to lay hands on someone, on prayer requests or send it to someone through a phone call or a written note. You have to release it and you get more. Many times, I would ask God to create in me more room to hold it.

Let none choose to live without this Holy Fire. It is God's will that every one of His children walk in all power to do God's work. God has made everything available for you to be fully equipped. It is God's will that you be filled with this fire. That's why all 120 believers received. None was left out but all of them received.

Who received and what were the preparations?

Those who received this baptism of fire on the day of Pentecost were only those 120 who were in the upper room: that is the 11 disciples, plus Jesus' brothers, Jesus' mother and the women (Acts 1:14). The baptism of fire is for both male and female. The Bible tells us that all of them devoted them- selves steadfastly to prayer, waiting together. So they waited. There is so much to say about waiting together. Waiting is for many a hard lesson but if people could Selah and meditate on how long and how many times the Lord waited for them, it might help them to get back in line and wait for God. How many years has Your Lord waited for you? How many times has He tried to bring you in His presence but you have kept Him on hold? In earthly terms, many people would be fired from their jobs if they put their boss on hold for too long but Your God is so patient that even though we kept Him on hold, He did not fire us but chose to wait for us. Behold, He stands at the door and knocks and waits for you to open the door! So how long, how many times did your God wait for you before you turned your life to Him? It might have been many years. Let His patience be your model. Learn to wait upon the Lord.

All the people whom God used mightily in the past and even today had to learn to wait upon the Lord. The disciples were commanded to wait and so should you. Yes, there is a time to be shut away. Even the Levites had to wait. "You shall not go outside the doorway of the tent of meeting for seven days, until the day that the period of your ordination is fulfilled. For He will ordain you through seven days." (Leviticus 8:33). It's not ministering first and then the fire. It is the fire first and then the release to assume your ministerial duties.

"The Lord is good to those who wait for Him, to the person who seeks Him. It is good that he waits silently for the salvation of the Lord" (Lamentations 3:25-26). This does not necessary mean to quit everything you were planning to do: job, school, etc. If God desires you to do so, that's even better but He will make it clear to you. To wait here means to tarry in God's presence, to wait on Him and not rush from before Him. It means to set a time when you get in the presence of the Lord alone, seek Him and spend as much time as you can with the Lord reading His word, meditating upon it day and night, worshipping the Lord and fellowshipping with Him. In doing so, you get to know God more and more to the point where you become a friend of the Holy Spirit and so become a friend of God.

So seek to know God more than anyone else, and more than anything else. In Him you will find complete joy, peace and rest. For those who are single and feel lonely, if you seek God diligently, you will find that loneliness is no longer there. Talk to God and pray. Spend time with God and learn to wait in His presence in silence and just abiding in Him. In doing so, you are drawing closer to God and you will find out that God draws closer to you. When you seek God, remember that He is also seeking you and is desperate for you. In seeking Him, little by little,

His kingdom will be great within you to the point that wherever you go, you will take it with you.

These dear saints who received waited in the right place, in Jerusalem, for the Lord had commanded them to do so. They were not in the world partying, nor were they gossiping. I don't see any of them who received the fire at the movie theater, nor at the Broncos' football game, nor at the park playing games, nor shopping, nor chatting on the computer, nor reading the newspapers. Though some of these things might be good and fun, they are not beneficial in drawing you closer to God. So the disciples waited, forsaking the things of this world. They knew there was something better than what they had for which they would need to wait. So they waited in the upper room, high above, seeking God's face earnestly and persistently, devoting themselves to prayer. Ten days, they waited on the Lord, not seeking His hands but His face. They had a determination; they made up their minds to wait upon the promise of the Father. They waited in the right place and they did not stand in the crowds of ungodly people! "'Therefore, come out from their midst and be separate' says the Lord" (2 Corinthians 6:17). You have to be in the right place of seeking God diligently before receiving this fire.

They were united and had their minds in complete agreement. So be united and in one accord. The fire is not given to those who participate in strife and sowing division of any kind. You might be saying: "Lord, you are asking too much!" Well, if you want much power, you have to sacrifice much! Remember, only God's pure vessel can be a channel through which this power flows. Only His dignitaries can bear this fire and bring this fire down. Be holy. Become His VIP. Serve Him in dignity. Purify yourself and like a true Levite serve Him. "For the Levites were more conscientious to consecrate themselves than the priests" (2 Chronicles 29:34). Yes, you will have to sacrifice the things that seemed dear to you which are not beneficial; you will have to give up all things that spiritually drain you and take you away from your Lover. All things, not some! You have to be willing to become a living sacrifice, broken and crushed before your Lord. The sacrifice must be an act of worship; you do it because you love God and want only Him not because of any obligation of any kind. The sacrifice must be brought before the altar, and the fire of God will be sent from heaven to burn the sacrifice.

As a Christian, a follower of Christ, you ought to walk in your Master's steps. Jesus' lifestyle must be your lifestyle. So pray, study the life of Jesus, let His life be your lifestyle and hasten to do all He asks you to do in His written and spoken word. Jesus was so full of power and fire all the days of His life. Search the scriptures and discuss them, tell people about Jesus and win souls. Wherever fire is, believers will speak in tongues, they will preach Christ and speak the mighty deeds of God with boldness. Believers who have received the baptism of fire are like a flame of fire. When they preach, people will be pierced to the heart (Acts 2:37). Sinners will repent and return to the Lord. Wherever the Pentecostal fire is, signs and wonders take place (Acts 2).

I will not stop here without telling you that your seeking the Lord and loving Him with all your heart will cause the enemies of God to rise up and attempt to stop you in your upward climb. What you are doing is perceived by them as committing a great crime, they will do all they can to stop you. Let them do their job, but also do yours: resist the devil at any cost and he will flee from you. The journey to catch the fire and to live a full life for Jesus is not a journey of honeymoons! You will be tested greatly and you must overcome. The tests are beyond comprehension, but you will be encouraged remembering that there are many who have been tested like you and passed the test and overcame. Also, God's grace and His love beyond compare will see you through it all. Fear not!

Who did not receive?

The unbelievers and those who were ignorant did not receive the fire until they repented. They did not receive for we see them asking "What does this mean?" (Acts 2:12). Drunkards did not receive this gift either since we see them concluding that the disciples were filled with worldly wine. When a man's mind is filled with evil, he believes evil reports about others because they fit in with his evil mind. In the same way thieves believe that all people are thieves and so hide their belongings wherever they are, so the drunkards concluded that the disciples were also like them full of worldly wine. Those who need alcohol, drugs and smoke to keep moving will not carry this fire, they will not be able to hold onto this Holy fire, it will burn them. You must not drink wine or liquor if you want to be a heavenly fire carrier. You wonder why the angel that appeared to Zacharias prophesied that John the Baptist would drink no wine or liquor. The answer is given in that very same verse: Because he was to be filled with the Holy Spirit while in his Mother's womb (Luke 1:15).

Mockers and scorners can in no way receive this fire. In my own experience I have found that people from almost all walks of life and beliefs can be touched and changed by this fire. But in any case where there were those scorning God and the gifts of the Holy Spirit, and with those whose pride dares say that this power is not of God, I found out that this fire was invisible to them. They could neither feel it, nor could they see it. God resists the proud but He gives grace to the humble.

Fire goes before Him,
And burns up His adversaries round about.
His lightning lit up the world;
The earth saw and trembled.
The mountains melted like wax at the presence of
the Lord,
At the presence of the Lord of the whole earth.
The heavens declare his righteousness,
And all the peoples have seen His glory.
(Psalm 97:3-6)

Chapter 4: Fire Invasion

After receiving the baptism of fire, there followed what I could call a "fire invasion" everywhere God sent me. At the coming of this fire invasion, iron bars and doors of bronze had no other choice but to shatter and open themselves. I saw a progression of firestorm that caused chains of bondages to fall off from many people, many of which were set free in the name of Jesus. There is no power in heaven, on earth and under the earth that can stand against the power of God. All problems, afflictions and oppressions disappear in the presences of God's holy fire. Words, theology, opinions of men all fade away before the Divine. When God comes, He takes over! All things serve God, nothing can resist the power of God. Nothing! Satan and all his demons and fallen angels tremble and quake before God Almighty. Mountains, great or small, disappear when the Lord passes by. There is no mountain that is great before God.

Many times mans' flesh is the only obstacle to experiencing the power of God and this is to their own detriment. If a man chooses to resist God in his own flesh, then he stays in bondage because God will not do anything against the will of a man. All prisoners can be set free except those who are self-imprisoned. It is not that bondages do not leave people. Bondages always leave people in the name of Jesus but I was astonished to see that many would not leave their bondages! Yes, depression and all stress melt like wax before the fire in the presence of God, His holy fire burns them all to cinders within seconds; mountains and all difficulties melt into nothingness before God, but people must not return to them in their minds, they have to walk away from them, they have to let them go and never pick them up again.

The continual burning

The never-ending holy fire would burn in me day and night. As this would happen, the inner man would not stop praying within. Even when I was outwardly engaged in something else at work, a powerful and fresh fire would constantly be burning within me. This fire was and is very strong, and I could not put it out by anything. It initiated a secret-silent prayer and worship ongoing within me at all times, even when I slept. Yes, I would sleep but my heart would be awake fellowshipping with God, singing to Him songs of love, praying without ceasing (1 Thessalonians 5:16). Within me the fire of love would be blazing like the seven lamps which always burn before the throne of God. The fire helped me to multi-task: working and at the same time fellowship with God as if in my private prayer closet. When I would get home from work, I would quickly change cloths and there on my knees under the power of the Holy Spirit I would lay down. This mighty powerful fire, so wonderfully vibrating, so dynamic, and so energizing filled me; caused everything within me to worship God. Down on my knees I would often say, "Oh, Lord I accept Your ministry of fire." I also prayed to God for His wisdom to know what to do with this fire.

I found myself no longer forcing my thoughts towards the Lord. In the past as I started seeking God, I had made a determination to be conscious of God's presence day and night but I had failed many times. This problem disappeared, however, with the coming of the fire. I cannot help but talk inwardly with the Lord all the time; I am conscious of His presence always and everywhere.

During this time I became less absorbed by the outer voice and became more sensitive to the inner voice. I also came to find that usually the mortal eye is corrupted and sees the negative, the problems rather than the solution. Many times people have problems because they pay attention to the things they can see, to the temporal when only the things unseen are eternal and real! What happens to men outwardly is less significant compared to what happens inwardly. Within, there can be real life or death. Thus a man should guard his thoughts as he guards his house against a thief or a robber! Thinking wrongly and letting oneself being discouraged by what they see with mortal eyes is trusting in deception. The things we can see are temporal while the things we cannot see are everlasting. The things we do not see are more real than the things we see outwardly. Oh, if only men would leave behind the temporal, live in the Everlasting, move in the Everlasting. That man would be not moved by what they see outwardly, rather than by what they believe. Man forms himself by what he believes. It is good to let go of any negative thoughts and fix the mind on Him who in the beginning was, is and is to come.

The fire of God has power to burn and purify and purge us. (Isaiah 4:4). Once you catch the fire, you will find that your acts, thoughts, works, words and all that is within you become purer every single day.

Miracles, signs and wonders

My prayer life reached a new level and I saw miracles of all sorts including physical and spiritual healing. I saw instant healing of all sorts and I was amazed at the miracles that were taking place everywhere in Jesus' name. Before my baptism in the fire, I was engaged in praying for the sick. Wherever I would see people who were sick I would run to them and ask if I could pray for them: at school, in a store, or in a restaurant. I would go to the hospital to pray for the sick on a regular basis. During that time, I saw how God was faithful in backing up His words, but victories were very few, very rare, and only happened once in a while. This was puzzling to me. The problem was that I would pray and try to force my faith to believe they were healed, but didn't really believe that they were healed. I tried to have faith and prayed many times, but they were not healed. Once in a while they would be healed! I wondered how I could have faith to believe for real. As I started seeking God diligently, I found that things were changing. To believe for real, to have faith without wavering you have to know God. It is faith obtained from fellowshipping with God. It is not easy to have faith in someone you know little about. The more you know God, the more real your faith becomes. Seeking and receiving the fire revolutionized my life at all levels. With the baptism of fire, new powers were released and the victories were astounding. God released boldness in me and a great confidence to know that the sick would be healed and it was so.

Miracles occur in Jesus' name by the faith of the one who is prayed for, but many times their faith arises within them through the one who prays for them. Those who are prayed for pick up doubts when those who minister to them are not sure if they will receive or not. When you are full of fire you are full of faith and boldness and through you this confidence and fire will cross over into them and cause faith and boldness to rise within them. Once this happens, a miracle takes place.

On July 23, 2004: During our first meeting which was such a small and simple meeting, all the people who came and were sick were touched by the power of God and healed. As I was getting ready for the meeting, the Holy Spirit spoke to me that there would be healing that night. He said that those who would cross through the door into the room where we met would be healed. Even though I had heard the Holy Spirit speaking this I did not share it with anyone. At the end of the meeting I asked anybody who was sick to come forward. God's grace is so great that one lady was instantly healed of ulcer problems according to the Word the Holy Spirit had spoken to me. Seeing this with their own eyes, many people believed. Miracles took place that night in Jesus' name and we all rejoiced and left the place fulfilled and overflowing with joy.

Oh, the ministry of the Holy Spirit! It is a ministry of power. It is a ministry of life. It is a ministry of glory. On January 12, 2005 while at a temporal job the woman, Aquilina, who sat next to me, was touched by this holy fire at first sight when we met. Within hours of meeting her, she was transformed not by words but by God's power. The Lord delivered her from all fear and depression and saved her whole family and restored her marriage. I remember the glow on her face! She was changed by Your glory, O God, and You filled her with Your Holy Spirit. She became a mighty warrior for Your kingdom. The next day after her conversion, she was filled with so much joy in the Holy Spirit that we could barely stop laughing the entire day. Around the same time, Bonnie P was instantly healed of back problems. The prayer was a very short and a simple one and most of it in silence. Mrs. Jackson was healed of problems in her right side. Evangelist Chester was healed of stomach problems.

A sister by the name of Mary had a problem with her right arm. For five days, Mary could do no work at all because the feeling in her right arm was gone and the arm was swollen, getting bigger by day. Through prayer, Mary was instantly healed by God's power. As we prayed, her arm started shaking vigorously, all the pain vanished and she started crying as she watched her own arm shrinking back to its normal size. This healing took place instantly. Feeling came back into her arm and Mary's arm was restored to divine health. I cannot mention all of the miracles that I saw and continue to see on a daily basis, just because of time. But I can tell you that all of the miracles I witnessed were instantaneous. We did not have to beg nor negotiate with the devil; Jesus gave us authority in His name to heal the sick!

Signs and other experiences always follow those who carry the heavenly fire. The Scriptures clearly say that many wonders and signs took place through the apostles' hands. We do not see many wonders and signs before the day of Pentecost. After being baptized with the Holy Spirit and fire on the day of Pentecost however, things started changing. Those who have received the baptism of fire see miracles daily because everywhere they go demonstrations of miracles and wonders accompany them. They are the fire and light bearers; they carry the kingdom of God wherever they go.

Miracles recorded in the book of Acts took place because the disciples had received the Holy Spirit and the baptism of fire. In the Word we see the healing of the lame man! He was lame from his mother's womb. Every day someone carried him to the temple gate called Beautiful to beg for alms. There he stood at the gate beautiful, his mind having been programmed since very young that He had to depend on the mercy of the people! But he was healed! You too, child of God, are not at the mercy of the world and its people. God who takes care of the sparrows, the ravens, the flowers and the cattle of the field is the one who takes care of you. This God who knows the number of the hairs on your head cares about you so!

Perhaps the gate was called Beautiful because when you crossed through the gate into the temple beautiful things were taking place inside. The lame man could not cross over since he had to stay outside so that he could beg. It was beautiful to the one who went inside, but not to the one who remained outside. That lame person only saw affliction, sickness, disease, and bondage. This lame man was at the gate every day, never missing a day. I am sure the disciples had seen him before because it was not their first time going into the temple. (In Matthew 24, we see them pointing out the temple buildings to Jesus.) They might even have laid hands on him before in vain. The disciples might have seen him even after they had received power from Jesus (Matthew 10:1). Jesus called the 12 disciples to Him and gave them authority over unclean spirits, to cast them out and to heal every kind of disease and sickness. Although He gave them power verbally, they could not help the lame man because they first had to be clothed in power from on high through the baptism of the Holy Spirit and fire. They had seen the lame man for 3 years while following Jesus, but they could not help him. Why? Because they were not yet clothed with power from on high. They had not received the Holy Spirit and the baptism of fire.

When they were filled with the Holy Spirit and tongues of fire had rested on each one of them we can see what a difference that made in their ministries. This time, something was different, something was new: they had been touched by the fire and they were filled with the flame of fire. We can see the confidence and boldness in John and Peter as they fixed their eyes on him and said "Look at us!" We can see the real faith that ACTS quickly as they say "in the Name of Jesus Christ the Nazarene walk!" I can imagine his leg popping up and hurrying to obey the word of the Lord as His word does not return to Him void. I am sure this miracle took place because the one who was prayed for had enough faith to believe, but his faith was awakened by the fire in John and Peter. When you carry the heavenly fire wherever you go people are awakened. The lame man, seeing they were full of Jesus, had no choice but to believe and was immediately healed.

People were filled with amazement and wonder when this miracle occurred. Jesus got their attention. This became an opportunity for Peter to preach and the people were touched to the core. Signs and wonders like this must occur at the hands of those who have received the fire, the power from on high. With the coming of fire, what was impossible becomes possible. In Acts 2:41 we see the salvation of souls and many miracles and wonders that God performed through the hands of the apostles.

This fire is the presence of the Almighty God, it is an unquenchable fire and nothing impure can stand before it. All things fall into order wherever the fire of God is. This is the fire we so desperately need now. It is the holy fire that penetrates everything and everywhere, knowing no boundaries. The baptism of fire to do all miracles is available for you and for me. This fire helps us do the works of Christ effectively. What do you think could happen if we all become flames of fire? Can you imagine what would happen if we all who are called by the name of the Lord rose up and shook the kingdom of hell, binding and casting out every demon in the name of Jesus? The captives would be set free!

The supernatural

The baptism of the Holy Spirit and fire is the beginning of a supernatural walk. Visions, dreams and prophecies and other experiences will accompany this baptism (Acts 2:17-18); we see the place where the disciples met was shaken (Acts 4:31); we see an angel setting the prisoners free (5:19-20); many visions were taking place (Acts10) and other supernatural experiences occurred. None of these miracles happened before the baptism of fire. After one receives the baptism of fire, there is such an outpouring of God's spirit that unusual miracles for healing, salvation, deliverance and wonders take place. Words that are a mystery to many will be made known to you by the Father.

Many of my nights were full of dreams and visions from God concerning things that would happen including disasters in the land, unknown things about people that I would not normally know. In many dreams at night I encountered God's angels especially, warring angels. I was shown mysteries about the nations and these were indeed God speaking because I would see the events days later in the news. Fire carriers will see the supernatural, they will walk in the supernatural and through them the supernatural will occur.

There are two supernatural experiences that I would like to share. These supernatural experiences took place in the ministry of Eava Currence whom I believe to be a great woman of God and also a fire carrier. On December 9, 2004 I was in Colorado Springs at the World Prayer Center. I had a beautiful time in God's presence in a chapel where many people came in to worship and pray. By the time I was about to go home however, something happened. I felt the Holy Spirit fire intensified and from experience, I knew there must have been more fire carriers in that place: whether men or angels of fire I don't know. All of a sudden, there was a change in the atmosphere; the fire was so great that I knew beyond a shadow of a doubt that God was up to something.

My eyes were closed seeking the Lord when I heard a woman of God checking the sound. She was to lead a prophetic worship service. It was time to go home but instead I decided to stop what I was doing and join those who had come for this prophetic worship service. My eyes were still closed but I kept hearing this woman of God checking the sound system, walking back and forth saying "They are here, the angels of the Most High." Even as she said such simple words, you could feel God's power was in the house and the fire of God was flowing like a river. I later learned that this woman of God was Reverend Eava Currence of Spiritual Restoration.

During the service we started by worshipping the Lord. The worship team was comprised of two people. Eava led the worship while her assistant sang. It was beautiful music as if sung by angels. It was not too long until the holy fire increased in intensity. The second the musician began playing the piano, the presence of God became so strong. Showers of fire were poured upon us. There I was on my knees loving the Lord, my God and my King. Eava, who very soon was about to fall prostrate on the floor before the Lord, had a quick chance to warn us that it was no longer her who was playing piano, to the amazement of many, but the piano sound would not stop. The beautiful music came out of the piano, yet all the people in the gathering were on their knees, including Eava and her assistant. No one was touching the piano; in fact no one was playing any instruments at all. Now who was praying the piano; who was producing those beautiful melodies? I did not have to open my eyes to believe this because I knew it was the angels playing. Nobody was singing but the music went on! The angels played for what seemed to be over an hour. It was glorious and I was greatly blessed.

Later on I joined the Eava Currence ministry as an intercessor. These experiences of the angels playing the piano in this ministry happened three different times on different days. I was there two times and I saw this myself and know it was the supernatural taking place. The second time when I witnessed this experience we were in a different room but still God showed up and we were all touched by God's holy presence among us. This time, angels played the piano for two hours! I believe those experiences are just a beginning of the supernatural in that ministry and other ministries of those who walk, live and move in the fire of God.

Since God gives the Spirit without measure, God's ambassadors will carry the fire wherever they go. They will be His kingdom carriers, taking and establishing the kingdom of God wherever they go. Wherever they will establish God's kingdom, His will shall be done there as it is done in heaven. Oh, how powerful this is! This fire will overflow through fire carriers and it will make an invasion everywhere they go because they cannot contain this fire within them.

Many, Oh Lord My God
Are the wonders
Which You have done!
As long as I live,
I will declare them among the nations
To the glory of Your holy name!
You Who are clothed with splendor
In the glory of Your majesty
Let all people hear what You have done,
Let them hear and tremble before You,
Let them be touched to the core,
Let them fall down and worship You

Chapter 5: A Journey With God

As far as I can remember, it all started when I was about seven years old. There must be something about this number that I have always liked! I was the seventh child among ten. When I turned seven however, something happened. Something sacred! Something Divine! At age seven, while I was playing with other children, all of sudden I started noticing the moon, the stars and the sky in a new way. They surely were there before but about seven years old, I saw them in a new and special way. It was as if heaven had visited me and I was awakened from sleep to know the Maker of all of these things. Yes, the moon, the stars and the sky were there before me, so beautiful and I was full of wonder and lots of questions. Was it that Heaven knew I was old enough and that the moment had come for me to choose life, eternal life? "Behold, I was brought forth in iniquity, and in sin my mother conceived me" (Psalm 51:5). Yes, children at that age can be saved.

It was in 1979. At that time my country, Rwanda, was extremely poor both spiritually and physically, living some very dark moments in its history. Everywhere I turned I noticed that almost everyone believed there was one true good God, unfortunately many would tell you that they did not know Him. They also believed there were other gods who could be good or bad and were not as powerful as the one true God. It was common for people to have names with attributes of the one true God and I was given the name Uwizera which means "The Believer". My parents had a farm in the country and our house was on the top of a beautiful hill and we owned the whole hill. Since my father worked in the city we would only be in the hill country once in a while during the weekends but later on we moved to the country for a few years. This hill was so beautiful and stood all by itself. From there, we had the greatest view and I spent much time there contemplating the beauty of creation, watching the sun set and trying to count the innumerable stars.

There was a big valley that separated us from the next hill and it was on this next hill that the catholic parish was established. These were the only missionaries I knew until I almost finished high school. These missionaries were catholic priests. My grandfather on my mother's side was a devoted catholic who welcomed them and my mother was considered by the people as a devoted catholic. She would be called on many times by local people to go and baptize someone if they were about to die. She smoked however, and like the rest of all other women around her she drank alcohol. This was not a problem for her church as most of these priests lived the same life style. When I asked my mother why they smoked, drank beer or went to see mediums, my mother would simply tell me: "Just do what they tell you and don't do what they do." I did and since I was a little girl, we never missed a Sunday service. My mother would always take us there. The only God our family believed in was the God preached by the catholic priests.

Beyond church walls

Something took place when I was about seven years old; something beyond what I saw at the church. Noticing the sky, the stars and the moon, I just started having many questions about who I was, where I came from and where I was going. I went to my mother to ask where I came from and who made me. I thought my mother knew everything but I was disappointed when she told me that she and my dad had made me. I was not satisfied. Still, my question remained unanswered. I kept wondering who made my parents and I was told my grandparents did. I ran to my grandparents to ask them who made them but their answer did not satisfy me either. I wanted to know the One Who is at the beginning of all things, the One Who is the Maker, the Creator of all things, the Giver of all life, the Source of all sources.

During this time I discovered that it was okay to ask questions to gain understanding and that it was okay to seek in order to know. God will answer you, and the true question will cause birth to its own answer. I realized at the moment I started questioning about the Maker of all things, my mother started reading the Bible to us at night before we went to sleep. We would all sit around the table where a traditional lamp was the only light in the room and hear mother read. What a marvelous night it was when the first chapter of the first book in the Bible was read! *"In the beginning, God created the heavens and the earth..."* Amazingly, after the reading, I had no more questions, I was amply satisfied! I had a different kind of desire to hear more about the word of God for His word alone quenched my thirst. I was so amazed by this story that the words my mother read stayed in my memory and became real. Yes, there was a God who in the beginning was and is above all things and who is so mighty that He created the earth and all that is in it! This God created me and my parents and my grandparents. This was God, the Creator of the moon, stars, heaven and earth. I understood that I am on this earth for a purpose: To do His will, to obey Him and to have an intimate relationship with Him...and that one day I will be with Him in heaven forever.

Asking God to put my name in the book of Life

From that moment on, I had so much interest in the living Word of God. However, since I did not know how to read, I would depend on my mother to read aloud so that I could hear this Word of Life again. The reading would take place maybe every other night. I counted the hours till the next reading. In my family, we had only one big black Bible. My mother could not read me the Bible as much as I wanted for we kept her very busy. We were ten children and besides that, my parents brought other relatives to live with us. They had to work hard to raise us. My father was a very successful man and he held different positions as a leader in the National Department of Education. My mother would be busy taking care of us. It was not possible for her to read me the Bible anytime I wanted. Besides, that book, the Holy Bible, was considered so holy in the house that she would not trust anyone to touch it. She kept it in her bedroom locked in a cabinet.

Two years later I was in my second grade of school. I learned to read quickly and I started reaching for this Bible and reading it with passion in the hiding place, however. My mother was not happy with that because most of the time I did know how to take care of it. Unable to wait till the next reading I would again take it anyway and run to the coffee plantation. Under the shade of this beautiful plantation I would lie down and read.

Something new happened to me when I read the book of Revelation and for the first time I found that there was a book about life in heaven, details about hell and other scary places; "And if anyone's name was not found written in the book of life, he was thrown into the lake of fire" (Revelation 20:15). I was filled with the fear of the Lord but also at the same time with joy and hope that I was given a chance to read this before I died. The word of God became so real to me. Within me I honestly said this prayer: "Master, God of the universe, let me have my name written in the book of life". After I finished this prayer, I also prayed for my whole family to be saved from hell.

From that moment on, I remember that I felt God was so real. When I walked, I felt Jesus was there by my side walking with me. I was so little yet I had a relationship with Him. Wherever I went ,I constantly beheld a picture of Jesus in my spirit handing me a white flower and smiling at me. Sometimes I would be gripped with fear knowing that God walked with me.

My interest in the things of God took a whole new level. A great hunger was birthed in me to know God more than anything. My mother kept taking us to the Catholic Church every Sunday. There again the word of God was read and I enjoyed it. Every night before we would go to sleep she would lead us in long memorized prayers and songs. Those memorized prayers repeated over and over again did not make much sense to me compared to the relationship I had started with God. But I would stay in tune and say them anyway because I always wanted to be where God was.

Orphanhood and backsliding

As I was turning about 11, my mother's health started degrading considerably. She was most of the times taken to the hospital, very sick, and since my elder brothers and sisters were either abroad or in boarding high schools, I would spend lots of nights at the hospital watching over her. In the morning I would go back to school. That was a hard time for me. Seeing my mother suffering I was afraid that I might lose her at any time. Talk about fear! I started living fear from Monday to Sunday. Like Job, what I feared most came upon me and what I dreaded befell on me. Both of my parents died of sickness, first my father in 1984, and then my mother in 1985.

There I was an orphan, at the age of 12! Oh, how awesome are the miracles of God. Let everything praise You, oh My God and my King – for in You the orphans and widow find mercy. Yes, I found mercy in You. I saw with my own eyes how You, oh God, took care of us and provided whatever we needed and even more. You who know the number of hairs on our heads, You who takes care of the flowers in the field and clothe them, the flower which is here today and is gone tomorrow, how much more will You take care of Your children whom You created in Your image. Yes, You alone took care of us.

Even though I had much fear following the sudden death of both of my parents, God sent a word to my family that He was our Father and that there would be no lack, that we would be better taken care of than those who had earthly parents. At my school though I suffered from the loss of my parents as many pupils could barely sit with me for fear that the same fate that fell on my family might be contagious and affect them if they sat by me; I however found favor with God and men. God gave me favor with my teachers and God raised true friends to stand up with us and support us. In school, my siblings and I excelled above the normal student. My brother, Jean

Damascene, who was the first born in our family, did all he could to raise us up and we all attended the best schools there were in Rwanda at that time. When I would feel grief coming over me, I would run to God in prayer. All the burden and fear would lift off quickly. God was so real and with us.

I learned to be responsible and had to take care of my little brother Philbert and my two sisters Chantal and Assoumpta at a very early age. I kept on going to church, but as I grew up I did not find much nourishment there for my soul. A veil still covered me somehow and the message preached by the priests was filled with shadows. I therefore lost that first love that had burned with fire inside me towards God and I became religious. It came to the point where I could barely say a true prayer and carelessly I slipped into the world and started living like everyone else.

By that time I believed that by being a good person, by following the rules, and by going to church once in a while that I would possibly enter heaven, totally ignoring the fact that Salvation is not the result of my own work. "For by grace you have been saved through faith, and that not of yourselves, it is the gift of God." (Ephesians 2:8). Oh, people – let there not be a "maybe I will go to heaven". You have to be sure. You have to know that your place in heaven is reserved. If you are not sure, that is an indication that you need to be saved. Come to Jesus and give Him your heart. You can respond to Jesus in any way you want by believing in Him but if you are not sure how to do that, say this prayer with me.

Dear Father God, because of what Jesus has done for me I present to You my prayer. With a sincere heart, I renounce my sins and I repent. I accept Jesus Christ as my Savior. I confess with my mouth that Jesus is Lord, and I believe in my heart that God raised Him from the dead. I receive the free gift of salvation. Write my name in the book of life. Thank You, Heavenly Father, for giving me eternal life. In Jesus Christ's name I thus pray. Amen!

When the danger of death encompassed me,
I cried out to God and said: "O, Lord I beseech
You, save my life!"
God from His holy dwelling place heard my cry
Not only did He save me from physical death but
also from spiritual death,
By the Holy Spirit's operation I was brought to the
cross,
There I learned that My Jesus was crucified,
Gave up His life so that I might have life.
On that cross it was written "Fully paid";
For in shedding His blood He purchased men for
God.
O, how can one reject this precious gift?
I walked towards the cross,
My eyes fixed on Jesus,
There I laid my burdens down.
I came to Him, and received forgiveness of all my
sins
I was thus born again into the kingdom of God.
The Lord spoke to me and said:
"See, I make all things new!
The old has passed away, behold the new things are
coming!"

Chapter 6: Rwanda Holocaust

I t was April 5, 1994 and I was in Rwanda. By this time I was a freshman at the Rwanda National University. I had been far away from God for about 10 years. I was no longer praying consistently; only once in a while. I was going to church but I went there because it had become a custom to do so. I was living carelessly; I guess you could have called me just a pagan! Wherever I was, however, I usually carried a small Gideon Bible in my bag. I would open it and read once in while and quickly closed it because each time I opened the Word, it would be speaking to me directly.

Since 1990, Rwanda had been in a political war. By 1994 it was the worst it had ever been. The after-noon of April 5th 1994, was unlike anything I had ever known to that point. The sky had a red tinge and the atmosphere was oppressive, something was going to happen, but what? During this time in Rwanda, many people including me, were not walking in the ways of the Lord. I was 22 years old and I had not heard anyone telling me about salvation through Jesus

Christ. People walked in ignorance, pride, disobedience and in hatred because of the tribal and political war that ravaged Rwanda. Extreme hatred had been growing between the two main ethnic groups in Rwanda, and they were at war with each other. These two tribes are known as the Hutus and the Tutsis. As the war grew worse, fear reigned in the hearts of many people... those hearts which were already cold and full of hatred! One could tell something bad was about to happen? It was very common during that time to be waiting for a bus in the city of Kigali and all of sudden see the crowds of people seized by panic running because they felt a bomb or someone was attacking them while it was all a hoax. "And the sound of a driven leaf will chase them, and even when no one is pursuing they will flee as though from the sword and they will fall." (Leviticus 26:36.)

During the Easter break from the University I visited my elder sister, Françoise, who lived in Kigali, which is the capitol city of Rwanda. Kigali was about 50 miles away from my school. She had just given birth to her first baby and it was exciting to visit with my niece, Bambine. Françoise was a very sweet sister. With Françoise I had never felt parentless even though I had been orphaned for years. That afternoon of April 5th, did I know it was the last time I would hold that precious little baby in my arms? That afternoon, did I know it was my last time to see my beloved sister Françoise in the land of the living?

Three unforgettable perilous months

On that day I snatched a few hours of conversation with my sister, but before evening came, I changed my mind about staying overnight. I felt pushed by something inside me to go to the hill country where my parents had a farm and where my grandparents lived. My sister and her husband could not understand why I changed my mind so quickly because I had planned to spend a couple of nights with them in Kigali. We argued without agreeing and finally I left them promising to come back again. However, within hours after leaving their home, they became victims of the Rwanda Holocaust and I would never see them again.

When I changed my mind about staying overnight, I called my brother, Jean Damascene, to ask if he would drop me off at the farm. He came and drove me to the country where he had to pick up his son. I had a great time visiting with my brother while driving to the hill country. I love my brother so much because he gave all to raise us after losing our parents; but like Francoise, I did not know that something bad was going to happen to him, that would cause him to be a prisoner of war, unjustly thrown in jail where he has been from 1995 to this day!

My 2 younger sisters, Chantal and Assoumpta, were already in the hill country for Easter break. My three brothers were also waiting for me but Jean Damascene had to go back to the city to join his family. He was already married with three young boys. Since we were a close family, there was such excitement to see one another again, and we were looking forward to having so much fun together. We threw a party for ourselves, celebrating this time of seeing each other after 3 months of being away to boarding schools. This party would turn into a tragedy in a matter of moments, however. As we were listening to the evening news, we heard that the plane of Rwanda President had been hijacked and brought down. The President was killed as well as some members of the congress and the President of Burundi. All the people knew that the president's death would be followed by something bad including the shedding of lots of innocent blood because an indescribable hatred had been growing between those 2 tribes that were fighting for power. During the war the Hutus were believed to be on the president's side and the Tutsis on the side of those who had attacked Rwanda since 1990. So the holocaust began; killings in which about one million people lost their lives in a period of 3 months.

After hearing the news about the president's death, my first thoughts went to Françoise and her husband, Vianney, and my little niece, Bambine. They were living in the capital where roads were immediately closed and where the first killings took place. Later on, a report got to us that shortly after the Rwanda President's death, Françoise and her family were taken by the army forces and imprisoned in a stadium. Later they were tortured and killed along with their two servants. A guest who happened to hide himself in their bathroom survived to tell us this story. Had I not gone to the hill country, I surely would have been killed as well! My God and My Father, I will never forget how Your powerful right hand rescued me!

From April to July 1994, lots of individuals died and mass killings took place. These were the most perilous months ever in the history of the world. I can remember the first time the killings reached the hill country where we lived! It was Sunday and we were in the last mass at about 11 a.m. The first killings in the hill country happened in the monastery where the crowds of men invaded and killed those who had come there to seek refuge. I can remember those days when houses and churches were burned with thousands of people inside. I remember those days when children, whose parents had been massacred, were left alone living day and nights in the parish cemetery without anyone to care for them. In those days before people would be killed, they would be given only two choices: either to dig their grave before being killed or to be killed and never be buried. I remember those days when we spent days in hiding, when I lost my siblings, family members and best friends. Days when sin increased more and more, and ruled in the whole country. There was no place to hide from that war. I believe the sin of Rwanda had increased to such an extent that even the ground and the rocks refused to hide those who ran towards them. As far as I could remember, it seemed as if the devil himself was ruling in Rwanda. Those killings reached every corner, every family; people met death at every turn. Those killings divided people, families, and broke up marriages and best friends. Sorrow and gloom could be seen everywhere during that time. There were signs in the sky and everywhere you looked. We were surrendered by uncertainty. "What was going to be the end of all the evil that was happening? Was there any hope," we wondered?

Surviving

*The cords of death encompassed me, and the
torrents of ungodliness terrified me.
The cords of Sheol surrounded me; the
snares of death confronted me
In my distress I called upon the Lord, and
cried to my God for help;
He heard my voice out of His temple
And my cry for help before Him came into
His ears. (Psalm 18:4-6)*

Though through many tears, dangers, loss of relatives, and loss of almost everything, I came out of that holocaust safely by fleeing to a neighbor country – Zaire/Congo, where I decided to start my life anew. The mass killings stopped in July of 1994. To me, Rwanda was but a country of horror, nightmares and bad memories. I vowed I would never go back hoping to find peace in a foreign land. However, a few days later, I thought I might have been wrong. True peace does not depend upon circumstances nor situations surrounding us. True peace is within and not without. It really does not matter where you try to go; without Jesus there will never be authentic peace.

If you are reading this book and you don't have peace, close it for a moment. Accept Christ Jesus as your Lord and Master. Think about Him and the peace He brings you. With all your heart, fix your eyes upon Him. There will be peace within; a peace that cannot be shaken regardless of where you are because the Prince of Peace is within you. Oh, the peace of God! The limited cannot take it away because it is unlimited. The world cannot take it away from you for it is from above. Live above, abide in Christ. Live above and let that peace that surpasses all understanding guard your heart. Peace - It is a covenant God made to His people. Yes, it is possible to have peace in the midst of turmoil; that's why the apostle Paul who was in prison could write to the Philippians telling them to rejoice always, to be anxious for nothing. "And the peace of God, which surpasses all comprehension, will guard your hearts and your minds in Christ Jesus" (Philippians 4:7). It is not that you have to move to another State, or country. Receive peace through Jesus, the Prince of Peace, and then you will have peace wherever you go. It is not that situation that needs changing first, but you must change first and then the situation will alter afterward.

Rwanda my beloved home – a country of thousands of hills became a country of bad memory! For over three years this country knew a terrible war and thousands of people found death from the very beginning of it. As if that was not enough, to mark the end of this war, ethnic killings took place in which an estimated of one million civilians were killed within three months. Rwanda is a very small country, comparable to the size of the State of Maryland. Those killings in such a tiny country could only be compared to the Jews Holocaust. I had to flee!

O Lord the Most High
You have granted me life
And loving kindness
You have given without judging
You loved me without condemning
And Your care has preserved my spirit

Chapter 7: Escape to Congo

It was a hot and dusty summer. There I was, a foreigner on the soil of Congo by then called Zaire. This was Rwanda's neighboring country. I was in the town of Goma following the Rwanda Holocaust and alone, without my family. I was not home when my family fled the war, alone in Congo I did not know where they were. Each of us had to run to save our lives. We were all scattered and none of us knew where the others were or whether the others were still alive! This was my first time experience out of the country and there I was homeless and without my family!

Thousands of refugees filled the country of Congo. In this new land the titles and respect that people had held in Rwanda or the wealth they had owned were of no value any longer! He who used to own a castle and the one who used to live in a hut were now treated alike! Oh, the riches of this world – not one person could take them from their home country to the neighboring country! How much more when we will have to pass from life into death? What can one take but life itself? On what basis will we value the greatness of a man in the after-life world? My friend Dora who was with me commented that it did not matter how great people were, what mattered was how they were going to start their lives anew in that foreign land. Oh, great God, help each person to invest his or her riches not in things on this earth that will pass away, but rather in heaven where neither wars nor thieves will steal it away.

Awaken

A hundred years is not that long,
Especially for those who live
by doing wrong,
It quickly comes but then you will
have your proof,
When your body stops its movement and it
does not ever again move,
Not because you're sick or crippled but
because you have taken your last breath,
And are now covered by the
shadow of death,
Who will you turn to now?
When earthly things you paid homage to, but
to the Lord you refused to bow,
How sad will you feel, my friend, in the end?
When your knees crumble and fall in the
Lord's presence,
Will it then begin to make sense?

(By Emmanuel Glory Ndongala)

In God's care on a foreign soil

Oh, the Love of God. For He loves and protects sinners! It is true that "The Lord protects the strangers; He supports the fatherless and the widow" (Psalm 145:9). How did I survive in this foreign land where I had nothing and knew no one? It is by God's grace and love that within the first month of my new life as a refugee I was given a job as translator to the American International Rescue Committee workers who came to respond to the crisis caused by the 1994 Rwanda refugees' influx into the neighboring countries.

It took us almost two hours to drive about a dozen miles because of the many dead bodies that filled the sidewalk of people who died fleeing the Rwanda war. The road was filled with masses of refugees. They looked just like a sea of people! This was the first day for the American International Rescue Committee team but I don't think they were prepared for what they saw.

On the roadside a hungry baby was crying next to its dead mother and no other relatives were in sight. From past the third roundabout, we could see thousands of tired refugees crossing the Rwanda/Zaire border. The noise of heavy weapons could be heard in the last battle of the 1994 war. As these refugees fled, walking many miles, the lack of food, water, and shelter caused cholera and other diseases to ravage through them without mercy. Numerous bodies were lying on the ground under the eucalyptus trees. The nearly dead joined the piles of corps, where they waited for death! These were my compatriots, human beings like me! Seeing them dying like dried grass made me wonder about what was happening to them after death.

Few people have ever seen such horrors. Human language is inadequate to describe the scene of abandoned and lost children crying everywhere; despair was on everyone's faces. There was horror and anger and finally silence. The rescue team was so shocked! Some of them called it "the road of despair" and others "hell on earth"!

That night I could not close my eyes to sleep. Instead, each scene of the horror of this war came into my memory. I had heard of wars, I had learned about World War I and World War II in detail, I had read about them but in my entire life I never thought I would live through a war. How wrong I was! In the year of 1990, a political-ethnic war broke out in Rwanda. As a result, many thousands of people lost their lives. The situation grew worse day by day. Many times I would find myself in a place where I could hear nothing but the sound of shooting and bombing. I found myself in places where many other people were killed, but not me. Why? Was I a hero?

During those hard times when the war was at its worst, I still had my pocket Bible which I never read. I would make numerous vows to God, "If only You could protect me now and deliver me through this horrible situation, I would thank You the rest of my life." Oh, the heart of man! How quick man's heart believe and quickly forget; quick to make vows and promises but also quick to break them. Quick to say "yes" and act in the "no"! As soon I would say my prayers, God would miraculously save my life but I would forget and move on with life as if I did not make any promises at all. I would take everything for granted and convince myself that I was somehow a hero.

As I found favor with my employers, people started calling me a hero. The world clothed me with its fame and titles and I became too proud. By then I believed there was a God but I would never turn to Him until I was in trouble, until I needed help. I would not come to Him until I wanted just to use Him. How can one person be so proud and still breathe? How vast is the love of God to preserve such a sinner as I!

I went on living in Goma, although I really wouldn't call it living because life is for those who have given their lives to Christ. Those who have not given their lives to Christ actually merely exist. In other words, they live in death! So I existed in the town of Goma. I first worked with International Rescue Committee helping refugees and it was during this time I found out that some members of my family survived the war and were in Bukavu, another town in Zaire. My young sister, Chantal, and young brother, Philbert, had survived the war. I brought them to live with me. My great sister, Daphy, was also in Bukavu with her family. My youngest sister, Assoumpta, was already married and she could not move to Goma to live with me. She stayed in Bukavu where another war found her in 1996. She would be lost in the jungle for nine years as a result of that war.

She became the subject of our prayer requests which God answered and we found her alive in 2005. For nine years she went through trials and tribulations but God's grace found her. And the best news of all was that she had given her life to Jesus in 1997 in the jungle!

My two brothers, Regis and Pascal, were also in Bukavu. When Rwanda later attacked Congo, these dear two brothers were shot to death because of who they were. Oh, the comfort I found in God! He is the God of all comfort who comforts us in all our afflictions and our grief. God is the only one who can bring you true comfort. Seeking comfort and sympathy from men only leaves deep holes, but when God is the Lord and Master of your life, He fills you with His peace, which causes all sorrow and sighing to flee.

In 1994, while employed at the International Rescue Committee in Goma, I met someone special who God has used to fulfill many of my dreams: Gregg Grunenfelder of Olympia, WA. Gregg became my boss while I was employed at the International Rescue Committee and we quickly became good friends. Gregg did not stay too long in Goma. After 3 months he returned to the United States but we kept in touch. Him and his wife, Catherine, gave to me generously. Three years later they would bring me to the U.S. and supported me and paid all my schooling fees.

Feeling the emptiness

What does it take for a man to acknowledge his Creator God? Wars and tragedies like the one I went through? Maybe a disaster like a Tsunami? What does it really take for a mortal man to be broken before God and return to God? Oh, God – You have made it easy for us to receive salvation but man has made it very hard, very difficult. Running and running away from God and then searching after the things of this world have made many lives very miserable. If only men would immediately obey God when they hear His voice! God does everything in His power to save people, to bring them to Jesus but He cannot do anything against their will for He is love. True love never forces. So God has been wooing us. May we stop running and quickly return to Him!

In spite of all I went through, still I would not turn back to God. And then another great war came to this foreign country where I had lived for over two years. It was in October 1996 and I was in Goma. During this time of war, I was so worried just like many ungodly people!

When this war hit Goma, the American team had left about two years before. When they left I was blessed to find another great job with The Lutheran World Federation. As far as my spiritual life was concerned, I had no relationship with God. I had money and a great job. In my outer world everything seemed to be going well. I even gained respect from many people because of the position I held at work. Inside me, however, there was only emptiness; things were falling apart within me. Truly, he who knows not God is empty.

Every time when I would wake up and my feet would hit the ground, I would hear an inner voice telling me to remember God, but I ignored it. To appease my mind I would make the Catholic cross sign "In the name of the Father, the Son and the Holy Spirit" as quickly as I could and then get ready for work. Besides this little prayer, I would never pray until there was a problem. I would go to church once in a while on Sundays. Though I was blessed with the riches of this world, I was empty and very poor. I lived in sin and in fear. My fear would increase day in and day out, especially on Sunday nights. The thought of the weekend being over and the end to all of that fun was gone made me uneasy.

With this emptiness in me I started seeking for something that would bring meaning to my life. It was God I was looking for, but I looked for Him in the wrong places. I made an appointment with a Muslim to see if she could take me to their gathering, and if it was good I had made up my mind to convert – but God protected me, the deceiving-Muslim spirit and this Muslim lady never showed up. I wanted to talk to people of other religions but I couldn't find many because God's grace protected me from them. I looked and looked in the wrong places but I would never look in the right one. I did not want to go back to Rwanda. We heard reports that even after the holocaust people were still being tortured, killed, and imprisoned everywhere. These atrocities were conducted by those who wanted revenge. So

I looked everywhere except in Rwanda. A country that sheds the innocent blood of its own people, I would in no way want to go back there! "Can any good thing come out of Nazareth?" (John 1:46).

Don't judge, don't despise. What is despised by man is highly esteemed before God. It is in that place I despised and dreaded where I met my Savior – Jesus, You take my breath away every time I think about how You saved me! I love You so!

Caught up in another war: Congo war

It was by then the end of 1996! The army of Rwanda had attacked Congo and the city of Goma and Bukavu were under heavy and terrible fighting. I remember sitting for the last time in my beautiful office, while all the westerners were planning to evacuate, leaving us behind. It was a terrible day. The war became so bad. We could hear shootings and bombings everywhere around us. There was no escape and there was no one to call. Besides the phones had gone dead because of the war. I had to run home and I made my way through fierce shootings. How hard it was to go through a war again and in a foreign country…but in all these things, God's love would never leave me nor forsake me.

Trust in the Lord and believe Him. There is no cliff too high and steep; no pit too deep; no ditch too long and narrow that He cannot use it as a way of escape for you. All things are subject to God. Listen carefully: No matter what situations you are in, no matter where you are: in the deep, in the midst of the fire, in a ditch, trust God. He has a way out of every situation for you. Don't complain and grumble. Watch and see how God will bring you through it. What has come against you is also a way out. That which the enemy sent your way to destroy you, God will use to save you.

Like the Rwandan war, when this Goma war started, our lives were in danger. Those who were believed to be on Rwanda's side (whether true or suppositional) were arrested. Chantal, my sister, had been arrested by the Congo army but we negotiated and they did not take her. I heard it on the way from work and rushed to those I believed were my true friends to see if they could hide her for me. To my surprise, one by one they refused to hide her even for one night. I cried, "Listen, that's all I have left; her life is in danger, they want to kill her." But no one cared, none were moved and none was willing for fear they would be killed or arrested if my sister were found in their homes. Today, I am glad that I found Jesus. In Him I found a true friend who remains, at all times and in all circumstances. Those who you call friends may come in your life, you might call them best friends indeed but lean not on them for there could be a day they might walk out the same way they came in. They may even leave you at the time you need them the most. The trials you will go through will determine who is your true friend. A true friend remains and loves to the very end. Jesus is a true friend. He remains. No trials, no situations, nothing can stop Him from being there for you.

I rushed back to the new apartment I had rented. The landlord lived in the same complex and he wanted us out. He said he did not want my sister to stay with us for she was certain to bring trouble. He told me "it is better for her to die alone rather than all of us". How incredibly selfish! He added that if I insisted that she stay, he would make sure all of us were out of there as well. But how could I let my sister wander around without shelter while I was given one? I cried to God and immediately a person I never thought would help showed up and offered to take her to her home for a while.

Evening came so quickly. As the battle between the armies of Congo and Rwanda became intense, many people left their homes to run away to the mountains. Goma became desolate! The landlord urged us also to leave; he was changing his mind by the minute. He said he did not want to be in trouble having Rwandese at his property. I looked outside and saw that a storm was raging. It was raining and thunder and lightning were everywhere. I'd experienced many flights from dangerous situations, but I wondered if I would ever make it out of this one! I was about to obey the landlord and run to the mountains, but the landlord did not want to give us back the money we paid for three months' rent. So we finally stayed because he did not want to lose that money! Many people and friends who ran to the mountains never made it back because they died or were shot during the war.

While everybody in that complex was hiding under their beds because of many shootings, my brother, Philbert, and I were forced by the landlord to climb up and stay under the roof, where we could hardly breathe and we were exposed to too much shooting and bombing. We stayed there all night long. Intense shooting and bombings were taking place nearby where we lived. I could not close my eyes. Instead, my spirit started wandering. Over a period of two long years I had run from the Rwandan war. And here I was again under the same war, and worst of all, I was in a foreign country. Through that noise of heavy weapons I remembered God – I was lost without Him. Very soon, there was no food nor any water, but God in His own mercy preserved us.

We spent about four days without communicating with my sister nor did we venture out of the apartment complex. My prayers were that she would not run to the mountains and indeed she did not. We survived this awful war and yet I was still seeking something that could bring meaning to my life. Lord, my Father, it was then at that time that we were introduced to a deceiving spirit of divination and witchcraft that claimed to have power from You; but You protected us from being involved and within a few weeks after this, we were transferred into Your kingdom of glory. I will never forget, my God, what You have done for me. Nobody was there except You. Your powerful hand never left us. You provided water and You alone provided the bread. You looked down from heaven and saw us wandering sheep; lost and about to perish because of ignorance and You said, "For My Name's sake, I will reach out to them." You had a plan. I will forever be thankful for the great things

You have done and I will proclaim Your glory among the nations.

Cleansed by
The fire of Your holiness
The fire of Your love
The fire of Your presence
The remnant will carry in purity and holiness
Your holy fire to the ends of the earth
Through them Your glory will be seen by all men!
Through them Your holiness will be revealed in all
the earth!

Chapter 8: Returning to Rwanda

By November 1996, the war was over in the city of Goma. Rwanda had taken the town of Goma and the war continued towards Kinshasa, which is the capitol of Congo. Like in the Rwanda war, many people, relatives and best friends lost their lives in Congo war. Many Rwandese refugees especially near Goma were brought back to Rwanda but many of those near Bukavu died. Bukavu was where my two brothers were shot to death and where my young sister Assoumpta was lost in the jungle for 9 years! I was among those who returned to Rwanda. I did not know what to expect when I arrived there.

On my way to the Rwanda border I passed by the United Nations' Refugee office, that huge building where we used to have offices and served refugees! It only served to remind me that the world's help was futile: Build hospitals for the sick, mortuaries for the dead! They can do good deeds but they cannot give eternal life – and now what could they really give? Only God gives! The world might try to give gifts, help here and there out of their kindness, but all of this is an empty container without refreshing drink. Nothing of this world can satisfy. Fulfillment is found only in God.

We had put all our efforts for over two years, working hard there, to serve thousands of refugees who lived in camps, but everything in those offices was gone...looted! All the files that were considered important were scattered everywhere, all the work destroyed! I stopped, stared and realized, "What a waste of time. Does not the Word of God talk about riches which are never destroyed? Have I ever invested there?" I kept walking and there I was at the Rwanda/Zaire border, the same border I had fled across a few years earlier! During my stay in Goma, I never thought I would go back home. That was an idea I had completely buried, not knowing what was awaiting me there! In fact if I knew, I would have come back earlier!

Something unusual on Rwanda soil

As my feet crossed the border and as I stepped in the Rwanda territory, I felt an unusual feeling, a powerful vibration going through my whole body, from the top of my head to the bottom of my toes. Within my heart there arose an inner voice that I could not stop. This inner voice was very powerful and its source seemed to be from eternity. The voice said over and over again: "Great and Mighty is God. Greatness, power, glory, victory and majesty belong to God!" This voice was unstoppable, I tried to control it but I could not succeed. This mighty voice inside me never stopped to tell the greatness of God. For many weeks, day and night, this voice proclaimed the greatness of God! I never questioned, I never doubted: This was the Holy Spirit speaking the greatness of God but how did I know it was the Holy Spirit as I was never taught about Him being real? Beloved, when God shows up you will be full of knowledge! When God showed up at the mountain top where Jesus had gone with John, James and Peter, His glory came down and the disciples were filled with the knowledge; we see Peter saying "Lord it is good for us to be here; if you wish, I will make three tabernacles here, one for You and one for Moses, and one for Elijah" (Matthew 17:4). Now, these patriarchs, Moses and Elijah, had lived hundred of years before but Peter knew who they were. They did not have to introduce themselves. When God comes to His people, they are filled with the knowledge.

This was God's work to bring me back home and to save me. How could it be that the place where I was wounded the most was the place where I would receive complete healing and salvation? How could the soil that drank so much blood be so filled with the presence of God? That one who crosses over to that land vibrates under the power of God. "Where sin increased, grace abounded all the more" (Romans 5:20).

Only God can take that which seemed to destroy us and use it as a vehicle to move us toward our destiny. Remember the Garden of Eden? Where the tempter, that ancient serpent Lucifer entered and caused Adam to sin and caused all of the human race to be conceived and born into sin? But, remember that there is also another garden, the garden of Gethsemane where Jesus defeated the power of sin. The apple tree in the Garden of Eden brought death to all mankind. On the other hand I see my Savior taking up a tree, a cross, and through the cross He secured salvation and eternal life for us all. Only God can use that which we call a problem and bring about a solution. To the one who sees, everything and every situation can be a way!

From the moment I crossed the border into Rwanda, the vibration and the inner voice would not stop – even when I got home. Wow! It was a miracle to be back home again. Seeing the place where I grew up, I thought I was dreaming! Looking at what used to be our farms and houses years ago, what a difference! Those houses which used to be filled with laughter and parties; those beautiful houses in that country of a thousand hills were empty, having been looted! Many people in that hill country were no longer there. You could only see a few people. No step could be heard, it was just me and God. That night, I knelt down before I went to sleep. I wanted to tell God how great was His work in bringing me back home, but I had not prayed for a long time and I did not know how to really pray.

Following the killings that took place in Rwanda war, something new happened in Rwanda. No matter how the evil one visited the hearts of many people and caused them to kill each other, God came down and visited Rwanda in a mighty way. I had not been home for two years and this is what I realized was new – the never-seen-before, the never-heard-of before: everyone we met greeted us in this manner "Yesu ashimwe" which means "Praise the Lord!" I wondered about this greeting! Not only the greetings but many things about the atmosphere seemed to be new. There were only a few people but they all glowed in an amazing way. They looked so humble, so confident and most of them walked with a purpose. There was hope in people's hearts. Many people had completely changed but how and why did they change?

Meeting God in the desert

Therefore, behold, I will allure her
Bring her into the wilderness
And speak kindly to her
Then I will give her
Her vineyards from there
And the valley of Achor as a door of hope
And she will sing there
As in the days of her youth
As in the day when she came up from the land of
Egypt
(Hosea 2:14-15)

Though the wars and holocaust were over in Rwanda, security remained an issue. Three years after the holocaust, many people went to sleep not knowing if they would wake up alive. One day, I saw my sister-in-law coming, tears rolling down her cheeks. I knew what she was going to tell me:

"Your brothers in Bukavu were killed!" Yes, I knew. That week, I had had scary dreams where I saw my brothers being murdered, and now the reality was before my eyes. After the loss of my parents, I had placed my total hope in my brothers. I believed they were my answers to everything. Who was I going to lean on now that those in whom I had put my trust were gone! For days after this event, I lived in total darkness. In fact, I could hardly make out a difference between a day and a night.

This is where I met God! It was the place where I had nothing and no one. That place where the world around you looks like an endless desert. Little did I know that it was in that desert, where I would find a precious present was waiting for me. I am talking about the hidden treasure that is described in Matthew 13:44.

Then the Holy Spirit came to touch me and comforted me. I became still and meditated upon all that had just happened to me and my family during the last few years. Was there any solution to this life of fear and wars and death? How could someone get out, or was there even a way out? I sought to know what in the world was going on! I sought with everything within me and I cried "I want out"!

I was sleepless that night. My sister Chantal had gone to see some friends but she did not come home for the night. I wondered where she was. Being away that late, that was not her at all. We used to talk and talk before we would go to sleep. It was getting too late and I expected she should have much to share since she had been gone all day long. I missed her but I became a little bit mad that she would spend the night somewhere else without telling me! She had gone to see Sylvia whose daughter was a best friend of hers before the war and they hadn't seen each other for over two years. I had heard about Sylvia – "that she was a woman fired up for God," but what did that mean? I wondered. As I figured my sister would not be back for the night, I went to bed and there in that room as I was still, I started having a fresh flashback of all that had happened to me over these traumatic years.

How I longed for a way out! In the midst of my meditation, the presence of the Holy Spirit filled the room. I was vibrating and trembling before Him. I heard His comforting, loving voice telling me: "Are you ready? Where would you go if your life is required of you tonight, like it happened to your brothers and sister?" I never argued, I immediately understood where I would go. The glory of God was in my room and I realized that I was a soul heading to hell if I did nothing! Friend, when you see the glory of God, you easily see where you belong. God is not a God of confusion. No, with God things are either white or black, heaven or hell; no questions. True, if you don't know you are going to heaven you are on your way to hell. In God, there is knowledge. Once you are saved, you know and you know you are on your way to that beautiful city. Up until that moment I did not have a personal relationship with God.

The presence of the Holy Spirit stayed and increased in my room. Again the Holy Spirit reminded me: "Can you remember the day when you said this prayer? 'Master, God of the universe, let me have my name written in the book of life." Yes, I had forgotten that prayer, but God never forgets our prayers and He does answer them all. At that moment, I cried because I knew I had wasted my life in the things of this world!

In the morning Chantal came home and, amazingly, she had been touched by Christ. She had spent the night at Sylvia's home fellowshipping. She looked so different and spoke only a few words. At night, I observed how she prayed and I could tell "Something profound has indeed happened to her!" She prayed in a different way. I did not hear any memorized prayers which were the only way we prayed. I could not hear any 'hail Mary'. I asked her what was the difference and she told me that she had gone to pray with the born-again Christians at Inkuru Nziza and I secretly planned to go there too but I had no clue of what was going to take place.

Thoughts of mine were lost in space,
Where I gazed at all and realized that nothing found
in this place,
Could be in likeness or surpass of my Lord God's
grace.
For we were lower than beneath him,
Yet He died for us and said I will not forsake them!

(By Emmanuel Glory Ndongala)

Chapter 9: Before the Mercy Seat

Rwanda – January 1997: True peace, unspeakable joy, assurance, radiance...that's what anyone could read so easily on my face. Back in my home land I found that which I had been looking for in the wrong places. As I walked down the stairs from Inkuru Nziza Church where for about two hours I saw an extension of heaven on earth, I said, "Truly, this is a new day, a new life, a new beginning." In that church I saw the power of God and it was there that I gave my life to Jesus Christ. That day was like no other because for the first time a full and meaningful life was born in me.

Oh, people! The distance between heaven and earth and hell cannot be measured by miles or any other earthly measure! About three hours before when I had walked in this church, I was of the earth and of the kingdom of hell. I was not a citizen of heaven but within a short period of time I was ushered into the kingdom of God by coming to Jesus. I came to Jesus and accepted Him of my own free will; nobody forced me. Yes, three hours before I was heading to hell but then I turned to God and I was on my way to heaven. When I entered the church I had no clue of what I would see. I had gotten there one hour before the service. I did not wait for Chantal to invite me. I invited myself. This was like breaking tradition because I was raised and my mother told me when I was very young that I should never attend any service other than the Catholic's, that it was a disgrace, and that I would be going away from God to do so. I broke that tradition and I did what was unusual. There were not many people when I arrived, but in they came, one by one. Amazingly, they all looked different from other people of the world I had seen so far.

The company of the redeemed

One by one they came. Very soon this building would be filled with hundreds of faces and they had something in common: they all radiated. "People," I wondered. No, they were more than ordinary people, but who were they? It was another kingdom for sure, a kingdom of love and freedom, and they seemed to know and care for one another! At about noon, they all started to sing the first song with passion, raising their hands. They were praying with confidence as if to a God whom they knew. These fearless warriors were worshiping in spirit and in truth and their souls were flooded with joy and love for one another and mostly for their God! They had something I wanted to have: love, peace and radiance on their faces and, unlike me, it was as if they had found what they were searching for and did not have to search any longer! "But how in the world can I be like them and have what they have," I wondered.

As they began to sing the worship song "How Great Thou Art," it was as if the world faded away. I kept wondering still who they were...people? No! More than that! They sang this song, prostrating on the floor as though before a king. One on one they communed with God. It was then that I gained understanding and I exclaimed "Saints! They are saints!" They were the redeemed, the saints who have washed their garments with the blood of the Lamb of God. In my upbringing, I had been told only a handful of holy people could gain the title of saints at the approval of the pope, but at that moment this theology was loosed on me and I knew these were saints, even though they were still on this earth. They sang like angels and they shone, radiating God's Shekinah glory.

They went deep into more worshipping and right there I was convicted of my sins. I realized that sin in my life was the reason why I was not like them. I tell you dear reader, receive Jesus and let Him take away your sins. Sins make a person ugly no matter how much make-up they might use. I looked, I trembled and I cried noticing my own exposed wickedness. I could not raise my hands to the One they worshipped for I was still a sinner. How could I lift up those unholy hands to a holy God? I could not imitate them for I knew something had to be done in me before I could lift up my hands like them. I made up my mind that no matter what it took I had to be among the company of the saints, the redeemed. They went on to sing about Jesus and they praised Him. During that time of worship, something took place in me, however. I don't know how but I looked and I found out that I was shedding tears and all the heaviness had lifted off me. I felt freer. I felt that I could travel in the air almost like a soap bubble. I shed many tears: tears about how I had wandered away from my Lord; tears of joy that it was not too late for me to be one of the saints; tears because I felt God's immeasurable love for me.

The two-edged sword

The Word preached by the minister was so true and full of fire. This word was a-sharp-two-edged sword as if spoken by the mouth of God Himself. The power of God descended upon me from heaven like fire at the preaching of that powerful word. I felt something like a blanket of fire and love enveloping me starting with my back where I used to have severe pain and then going throughout my whole body. The Master touched me. He washed me. He sanctified me and He justified me. The presence of God came on me so mightily and for the first time I tasted heaven. All worries, fear, problems, unforgiveness, darkness and sickness vanished instantly.

I had been suffering from terrible back pain for years and had seen doctors who could not help me at all and things had gotten worse. As the Word was being preached, I felt a lot of heat throughout my whole body, especially on my back. Suddenly my back was healed and all the pain disappeared. Before the service was even over in my heart I had already given my life to Jesus. Jesus was (and is) so good. He is so full of a kind of love that is not found on this earth, please don't refuse Him.

I was not sure if the minister would give an invitation to receive Jesus Christ. While I was wondering about this, there it came; an invitation to receive the Lord. Why did it take me so long to come to Christ who is so loving, lovely, meek, tender and mild? Who is powerful and mighty enough to save? Only the Lord! As the invitation was being given, even though I was sitting all the way back of the church, I stood up without being ashamed and begged to receive Him. Wearing a black skirt and a yellow vest I walked to the front and I accepted the Lord Jesus as my Savior. From that moment on, my life has never been the same again. All fear, all burden, all pain from the wars, all sins were laid at that altar and I would never pick them up again. There at the altar, at the cross, I received Jesus Christ. Before I left the altar, the preacher quoted the following scripture: "In that day you will know that I am in My Father, and you in Me and I in you" (John 14:20). In reality, I did not know what he meant, but what took place from that moment through today confirms what the minister said: He is within me!

Away with the old!

God means what He says. The moment I freely opened the doors of my heart to Jesus, He moved in to abide there forever. My heart became His temple.

He came in and I became a different person. The second I stepped outside the church, I knew that I was different. I could not help seeing two pictures before my eyes: the old Christine and the new Christine. Now I understood what Jesus meant when He said, "Unless one is born again, he cannot see the kingdom of God" (John 3:3). Yes, I was born again and I could see the kingdom of God! At that very moment if you had asked me to give up my Jesus in exchange for all wealth of this world and its entire kingdom, all the gold and silver of the planet...I would have laughed at you and told you "No, thank you. Only, give me Jesus!"

As I stared at the path, I realized that I was not alone. He was with me, my Savior Jesus. I could feel that He would walk with me. I did not have any means of transportation but I did not see any need to worry about it walking with Jesus. I was so filled up with the fullness of God; I did not have any want, I who used to be a seeker and had many questions that puzzled me! I was about to walk about a mile to the bus station but at that very moment before I could even make the first step to go, a nice car, like brand new white pulled in front of me. A driver whom I did not know opened the door for me and said he had just come to take me wherever I needed to go. I knew he was sent by God and I requested him to drop me at Sylvia's supermarket store. Now Sylvia is the godly woman who had led my sister a day before to Christ. Sylvia then warmly welcomed me, she had me come in her office. I sat with her for what seemed like 3 hours and during the entire time she told me about God. She told me about the greatness of God. I had goose bumps all over me and I was shocked that I had lived my life in total ignorance of who God truly was. Was God so real that a person could be a friend of His, have a relationship with Him, talk to Him and hear Him? I was astonished that a person could hear the voice of God. Full of the Holy Spirit, Sylvia told me about Jesus and she explained to me the scriptures.

God was with me and before I expressed the desire of my heart, it was as if He heard my inner voice and He responded: "It will also come to pass that before they call, I will answer; and while they are still speaking, I will hear" (Isaiah 64:24). Before I got home I encountered miracles after miracles, and it remains so to this day. Jesus came into my life. I could see Him moving on my behalf in every situation. His love for me is always there and was there even when I was a sinner, but by the bad choices I had made, my eyes were blinded and they failed to see the truth about His love.

That day, I gained the understanding that during the entire service I had been before the mercy seat of God. Before the mercy seat I was fully forgiven, fully accepted, fully restored and fully saved. God made all things new in me. He gave me new eyes with a new perception. When I looked I would see the beauty of the Lord on everything and on everyone. I noticed the beauty of the sun, the sky, the stars and the moon in a great way like when I was a little girl. I could see life in them. When I would meet people, I would testify about the little I knew about my Savior. We all need to learn to see through the eyes of God! When you see through His eyes you will see things differently. In His word God says "As I live, all the earth will be filled with the glory of the Lord" (Numbers 14:21). Are you seeing God's glory or are you instead finding faults and shortcomings in people you meet? Are you only seeing hopelessness, dryness and problems? If so, then it is time to see the whole earth filled with the glory of the Lord. The only way to do this is to see through the eyes of God.

From that moment on I started receiving God's blessings including favor and grace upon grace. There came a song of praise within my heart. I started hearing the voice of the Holy Spirit, Who also taught me the Bible and I started to commune with Him intimately. Within a short time after being saved I had almost finished reading the Bible and I was shocked to see the truth it carries and the power therein to rule and reign with Christ. I could not help myself from witnessing to people and I will continue to do so until I go to my heavenly home. I am glad to be part of the kingdom of God and friend...I encourage you to be part of it too.

It is Jesus Our Redeemer,
Boundless, Divine Mercy!
A battered reed He will not break,
A smoldering wick He will not put out.
He will not extinguish the hope of man.
He will not harm the helpless.
His was a mission of redemption,
He accomplished it and finished strong,
Now those who believe and receive Him;
Are freed from their sins,
Washed by His own blood,
Forgiven, sanctified and justified
Theirs is eternal life;
They will enter by the gates into the city,
The New Jerusalem to share with Him the joy of
heaven
Forever!

Chapter 10: Jesus, No Other Name

There is something different about Jesus. He is not just a good man. He is a mighty God, a Savior who came to save the human race from their sea of sin and deliver it into the kingdom of glory. Jesus is great, powerful, glorious, victorious and O how majestic is His name in all the earth! He is incomparable to anything or anyone else. There is none like Him in heaven, on earth, or under the earth. Jesus – what a beautiful and matchless name! "For who in the skies is comparable to the Lord? Who among the sons of the mighty is like the Lord? A God greatly feared in the council of the holy ones, and awesome above all those who are around Him. O lord God of hosts, who is like you, O mighty Lord?" (Psalm 97:6-8). There is no god, no hero, no good person whom we can compare to Jesus. The only One who conquered death, the only Master over the grave and the first one to rise from the dead is He. I cannot help but tell you about my Jesus. He is beautiful, full of grace and truth, He loved and still loves sinners. In fact, He died for them while they were still sinners.

He is the only one who will love you to the very end. Jesus lived a sinless, perfect life and yet He bore the sins of mortal men and clothed them with His own righteousness. Oh, Jesus, my Jesus! No one is like Him. He is unsurpassed in majesty, power and authority.

Jesus! He is the only one who tells you "Turn to Me and be saved, all the ends of the earth;" (Isaiah 45:22). Jesus our Savior! He is our Savior from sin, from sickness, from our enemies, from all that is against us. Jesus! Such a powerful name before which all of the evil hordes flee. It is such a powerful name before which all names whether in heaven, on earth and under the earth will one day bow down and say "Surely, He is Lord"! The name of Jesus is such a powerful name that even saying "Jesus" one time leaves you changed. It is such a mighty name that even thinking about Him can free you from all evil.

Jesus is the only one who is worthy and trustworthy. In the book of Revelation John was shown the book with seven seals in heaven, the angel proclaimed and said "Who is worthy to open the book and to break its seals?" And no one in heaven or on the earth or under the earth was able to open the book or to look into it. John began to weep greatly because no one was found worthy to open the book or to look into it but one of the elders said " Stop weeping; behold, the Lion that is from the tribe of Judah, the Root of David has overcome so as to open the book and its seven seals." (Revelation 5:2-5)

Jesus! His dominion is an everlasting dominion which will not pass away; and His kingdom is one which will not be destroyed! All the kingdoms (there are many) of mighty men, heroes, kings, princes and those of other gods whether on earth, in the heavens or under the earth will be utterly destroyed at the appointed time; but His kingdom will last forever. Dear one, be part of His kingdom while it is still possible. You will never have regrets if you know and serve Jesus… no regrets at all. None!

The invitation

The Lord wants to save everyone. He has talked to you through situations and circumstances and in many other ways, but He is such a great lover to you. He gives you a free choice, you can choose but to accept or reject Him. He will never force anyone into a relationship. You know why? Because God is love and true love is never a command. True love never forces against one's own will. True love never steals nor takes without permission. A demon might possess somebody by force, but God will never force His love on you because He is all Loving and a loving heart never forces.

Jesus said, "For apart from me you can do nothing" John 15:5. Philippians 4:13 says, "I can do all things through Christ Who strengthens me." Friend, let me challenge you: What will you freely choose today? Tomorrow may never come, or this might be the last time you have a chance to repent and unite with the One who loves you with an ever-lasting love. So repent! Repentance is not an apology and then you can repeat the same action again, as usual. Repentance is not about repeating the same habits over and over again. If you repent of your sin today, it should not be repeated again the next day because once you repent you change. If there was no change, it was not repentance; you were more than likely just feeling sorry for your actions.

Accept your salvation at any cost. Don't wait. Never meet death nor the grave without having Jesus on your side. God wants to make it a simple thing for you to accept Him and receive. If you don't want to be saved then let all that must be done to you be done so you will finally say yes to God. There are many who ask if God is love then why does He send people to hell. Let's be clear about this issue. God loves people and He is not sending anyone to hell. "Behold, the Lord's hand is not so short that it cannot save; nor is His ear so dull that it cannot hear. But your iniquities have made a separation between you and your God, and your sins have hidden His face from you so that He does not hear" (Isaiah 59:1). The sin that people choose to harbor in their lives is that which sends them to hell. In the case where a prodigal child chooses to disobey his parents and get in the wrong company, and start taking drugs while he was warned, and his parents did all they could to prevent this but the child disobeyed and chose to rebel, who is to blame? If parents cannot be blamed for that situation, why would we blame God when His children rebel? People, we need to repent and be saved today because tomorrow might not come.

I am sure you don't want to go through the horror I went through to be saved. You can be saved right now. You might say that you are not a great sinner because you don't do this or you don't do that. It does not matter whether you are a great sinner or a small one; both sinners will end up in hell if they don't repent. Not even one unrighteous act or thought will be allowed to enter into heaven. How many unrighteous acts have you committed or how many impure thoughts have you had? Who can be saved since it seems impossible to be completely perfect? Who can live a sinless life by his own strength? Who is the one who will dare to stand before God in his own righteousness and say "Receive me to heaven because I deserve it"? Who is the one who is not going to need Jesus by his side as the day comes when we will stand before the great white throne of judgment of God, the Righteous Judge? None – not even one. All will need Jesus! Those who confess Him before men, He will confess them before the Father. Those who deny Him, He will deny them. Judgment is coming. On that day, there won't be any soul missing. From the children murdered through abortion or those who died in other ways still in their mother's womb to the oldest person who has ever lived, none will be missing. All the dead, whether great or small, will be brought before the judgment throne of God. There won't be anywhere to hide for on that day the earth and the sea will give up the dead in them; death and Hades also will give up their dead to be judged.

Who will pass the judgment of God in his own righteousness? Who will? I am sure God's love is so great that He would desire to save all people but He cannot violate His nature as a Righteous Judge.

Righteousness and justice are the foundation of His throne. How does someone make it to heaven then? Your ticket to heaven is Jesus Christ. Heaven is a place you enter because of what Jesus has done for you, not because of what you have accomplished. Only Jesus was found blameless. By receiving Him, He gives you the right to become a child of God and He clothes you with His own righteousness.

The character or soul of man will never die, not even after this life! The life one will live after death is a continuation of the life started here on earth. Those who have Christ in them are saved and they will go from glory to glory, from beauty to beauty, but those who do not have Jesus Christ are lost. These lost souls will go from worse to worse and there is no chance for them to improve their character for righteousness after death because they have rejected Jesus Christ. The character of a man must be changed while he is still on this earth. This is only possible when they receive Jesus Christ as their Lord and Savior. I am glad that God would make it easy for us to have the mind of Christ and His character and not our own.

Cancel the reservation from the pit of hell

Salvation is a free gift and God sends the invitation to everyone. When people receive it and accept it, they are on their way to heaven. When they reject this invitation, which comes from the Creator, the One Who created them, they are negligently making their reservation for the pit of hell. We choose the pit over heaven and start decorating it with all we do outside of God's will. We miss heaven because of own free will, free choice and on our way to hell we go. In this situation, is anyone else to blame except us? No one but us! I wish that people would pause a minute and calmly consider this situation. If only they would take a minute to see where they are heading! If you were asked to identify your eternal home (heaven or hell), what would your answer be? Is it "I don't know" or "I am not sure"? If yes, then that means you don't have Jesus.

Just as no one can have an audience with a king of a nation and not remember that event, so no one can have Christ in him and be confused about it. It is important that anyone reading this book who is not yet saved heed the voice of the One Who is calling him today. Jesus is the Way, the Truth and the Life. No one makes it to heaven except through Him. Do not trust the voice that says you can be saved tomorrow, for tomorrow might not come. Be not overtaken by the things of this world for not even when you have an abundance does your life consist of your possessions. *"The land of a rich man was very productive, and he began reasoning to himself, saying, 'What shall I do, since I have no place to store my crops?' Then he said, 'This is what I will do: I will tear down my barns and build larger ones, and there I will store all my grain and my goods. And I will say to my soul, 'soul, you have many goods, laid up for many years to come; take your ease, eat, drink and be merry.' But God said to him, 'You fool! This very night your soul is required of you, who will own what you have prepared?' So is the man who stores*

up treasures for himself and is not rich toward God'"
(Luke 12:15-22).

"...Make yourselves money belts which do not
wear out, and unfailing treasure in heaven, where
no thief comes near nor moth destroys. For where
your treasure is, there your heart will be also" (Luke
12:33-34).

From heaven
A heavenly fire comes
It cannot be consumed
It only consumes

An empty vessel I come
Fill me O, Eternal Consuming Fire!
Fill me with this blazing heavenly fire

Chapter 11: A Flame of Fire

At the new birth those who give their lives to Christ are to a certain degree touched by God's holy fire. Believers can receive as much fire as they are able to pass on; also believers can receive the measure of fire according to their spiritual level, their thirst and hunger for the things of God; and sometimes according to the intensity of the fire in the place where they fellowship. The fire those new believers receive needs to be nourished in order for it to grow; if not nourished it lays dormant in peoples' hearts and eventually goes out.

Though many don't receive the baptism of fire at the new birth, each child of God receives the fire from God at their new birth. For some it is a weak, lukewarm fire; for others, it is a fire that has been buried and the only evidence of its existence is smoke rising up. Beware of the fire whose only evidence is the smoke! Smoke does not bring the light!

For others, they have received the baptism of fire, which is a mighty, intense fire that blazes, burning wherever they go. Every disciple of Christ wholly dead to their flesh is a candidate for a baptism of fire. Believers who are baptized with this fire are totally immersed in the fullness of God's holy fire to the extent that they eventually become a flame of fire themselves.

A flame of fire gives birth to a flame of fire

Who makes His angels winds, and His ministers a flame of fire" (Heb 1:7).

Those ministers who have become a flame of fire are the fire carriers and the fire starters. Wherever they go, in season or out of season, they set people on fire for God. In the same way a person who is cold can be warmed up by the fire, many people whose hearts are cold can be changed and warmed up when they come closer to the fire carriers. The cold-hearted will be touched by this fire and they will be changed.

Ministers who have become a flame of fire become more effective in their ministry and they spiritually give birth and produce fruits which are also flames of fire – for trees bear fruits after their own kind (Genesis 1:11). Therefore, those who are born again under the covering of a minister who has become a flame of fire are more likely to receive the fresh fire quickly. Receiving the fire does not have to do with how long you have been saved. In Matthew 20:1-16, laborers who were hired in the morning received the same wage as those who started in the afternoon. In the kingdom of God, those of us who start first and those of us who start last have equal opportunity to receive from the Father.

That every minister were a flame of fire! The Gospel of Jesus Christ will spread like a fire that burns the forest in a dry season and like a flame that sets the mountain ablaze. He who tries to minister without this fresh fire will be ministering in his own strength and flesh. Flesh can only give birth to flesh, but that which is born of the Spirit is spirit. All of God's true ministers need to become a flame of fire! They need to be full of zeal, holy passion and anointing so that nothing can stand before them. We desperately need to be filled with the Spirit of burning and have absolute authority over all the power of the devil according to the Word of God (Matthew 10:1; 18:18). A true minister has power in Jesus' name to bring permanent transformation into people's lives wherever they go.

If you are a believer who works with sinners but they are the same day after day, this is a good indication that you need a blazing holy fire in your life. If you are a minister of the gospel and sinners are coming to your church and leaving the same way they came in, this is a good indication that the fresh fire was put out in the house of God! 'Fire shall be kept burning continually on the altar; it is not to go out" (Leviticus 6:13). Oh, Holy God – unveil the eyes of every minister of the Gospel. Help them to bring the fire back and to keep it burning on the altar! Only then will they preach the Good News. The Gospel is not merely a word. The word must become acts through signs and wonders.

A flame of fire penetrates everywhere

Seek God, live and move in His presence. Wherever God's presence is, there His fire will burn also. Daniel saw the Lord, His throne was ablaze with flames, and its wheels were a burning fire. A river of fire was flowing before Him (Daniel 7). It is the presence of God that will bring the fire – the fresh fire. This is a consuming fire that knows no failures and consumes all chaff. You ministers of the Gospel of Jesus Christ, live in that fire. Act from the fire and minister to God's people from the fire. Be a flame of fire and you will see many who live in darkness being transformed because such a flame of fire from the blazing throne of God will travel through every dark room within a believer's life and they will be full of light.

The days that are ahead are evil; only those of us who keep this inner burning fire will overcome! The never-heard-of wickedness is taking place throughout the land. New demons are being sent out by satan. Satan is inventing all sorts of new lies, he forges new wickedness day and night, and he takes no rest. At the same time God is doing a new thing in us so that we might be able to withstand the battle, and not only hold our own ground but also launch attacks, setting free the children of God who are being held in the enemy's camp. There is a need to be a flame of fire – being a flame of fire will bring transformation and hope wherever God sends us!

We have heard of men and women of God who even in this age shook this world simply because they were flames of fire. Among them we see the 120 who were in the upper room, and it is through them that the Gospel of Jesus Christ is spread even unto the ends of the earth. We have heard of mighty servants of God like John G. Lake who received this baptism of fire and from then on had a cutting edge healing ministry where 100,000 investigated healings took place making Spokane, Washington the healthiest city in the world. We have heard of Smith Wigglesworth who walked in such an astounding measure of anointing that he would demonstrate the power of the book of Acts wherever he went. We have heard of Maria Woodworth Etter who walked in such a powerful anointing to the point where people would be struck down, fall and freeze under the power of God for 50 miles around without even knowing there was an evangelist in town. They would lay there for hours and have wonderful visions of heaven, angels and hell and walk in the supernatural power of God. Many would go into the ministry or become evangelists. We have heard of Kathryn Kuhlman who walked in the love and power of God. Healing miracles were astounding in her revival meetings. These men and women of God knew what it was to be filled with the spirit of God and they were all baptized with the Holy Spirit and the fire. They themselves were flames of fire and they made the power of God known to all. I don't have room enough to mention them all, but other men and women of God such as Benny Hinn, Todd Bentley, and David Hogan are serving God with this fresh fire.

Benefits of heavenly fire

Fire cleanses by burning the old away. When I gave my life to Jesus Christ, so great was the intensity of the fire of God that instantly, darkness and horror faded away. Old habits in me burned away one by one. I was the greatest sinner of all and the most hypocritical person that I have ever known. God touched me and His fire burned away the old. When I got home I was a changed person. That very same day I got rid of all the ungodly music I had. You have to understand that nobody had told me it was wrong to listen to them but the desire to do anything that took me away from Jesus was uprooted in me – roots and fruits were burned away, praise the Lord! The old life must be burned away every day, therefore you must walk in the fire everyday. We go from glory to glory. The glory of yesterday can no longer be the glory today. When you walk in the fire of God, the old will be burned away and you will walk in the new every day of your life.

Fire consumes fear. With the coming of the fire, fear cannot stand. In the Bible, God says it over and over again: "Fear not." We therefore know that fear is not from the Lord. Partner not with fear; give not in to fear in your life, not even for one minute. Make no friends with fear for he is a wicked friend. Seek no consolation from him and do not believe in him. Fear is a demon, not a partner. Do not dare to associate with him. It is useless to let one's thoughts be taken by fear of the future or of any sorts. God alone gives life and He holds everyone's life in His hands!

Since God gives life, hold onto Him and trust that He is not going to give you over to something that will destroy you. God alone is sovereign, His sovereignty rules over all! All things are subject to God and they can be moved at His wish, "For all things are your servants" (Ps. 119:91). You see, there is no reason to fear! Fear wants to steal the joy of the Lord that lives within you and wants to force you to lie under the bed of depression and affliction. Dear child of God, it does not help to cooperate with this enemy. In earthly terms, will the king's favorite child worry about how he will pay his bills for telephone or rent, as long as he lives with the father and has an intimate relationship with him? If that thought does not enter even into the minds of the children of kings on this earth, then what convinces the children of God (Who is the King of all kings) to believe the lies of the enemies that something bad is going to happen, that God has forgotten them and will not care for them?

Fear and pain are both signals, warning signs. When you detect fear before you make a decision, usually this is a sign, an indication that the decision is not of the Lord but of the evil one. Like fear, pain is also a signal. Unlike fear however, pain comes after committing error. Therefore, fear is a sign that you are about to err and pain is a sign after the error was made. With the coming of fire in the believer's life however, fear flees away. You can be afraid until you step into the fire. When you are immersed in the fire of the Living God, fear, along with all of the chaff, are consumed.

Fire is very powerful. It is the fire that brings light. It is the fire that absorbs water, it is the fire that boils water, and thus fire is master over the water. It is the fire that burns the chaff and dried branches, wood, hay and stubble thus fire burns that which is no longer good. Wood and hay and stubble represent: bad character, a mind that is not of Christ, and the personality from the flesh. Man's character can be transformed but it never dies. The day when the trumpet will sound and your life is required of you and you die, you will not leave behind your character. Your character never dies and it will follow you and this very character will drag you to those who have the same character as yours: the unholy will be with the unholy and the holy with the holy! What then if your character and your mind are not now of Christ? If you don't love Christians now, you will not love them when you die. If you persecuted the children of God in this life and you die without repenting, your character of hating them will follow you in the after life. There will be a separation of these two groups.

The life you will live after you die is a continuation and a prolongation of a life already started on earth. That's why in the book of Daniel it says that *"The wicked will act wickedly"* (Daniel 12:10). John the Revelator goes even deeper and says that *"Let the one who does wrong, still do wrong; and the one who is filthy, still be filthy; and let the one who is righteous, still practice righteousness; and the one who is holy, still keep himself holy"* (Revelation 22:11). The righteous will be more righteous in that life, but the wicked will act more wickedly.

When you receive the fire, your bad characteristics will die one by one as you allow yourself to live and walk in this fire. These bad characteristics will burn because they cannot stand before the Consuming Fire. All chaff must be burned. When you allow this fire of God to touch you, it will purge and purify you (Isaiah 6:6-7). You will receive God's holiness and you will walk blamelessly in the ways of the Lord. This is a mighty fire from God's throne room and, bride of Christ, this fire sees to it that the dried and dead branches are cast into the fire and are burned to cinders. Yes, the branches that are no longer delivering fruits will be cut off and through this pruning new ones will be born and bear new fruit.

The benefits of God's holy fire are many. In my experience, I have found out that the fire intensified a new understanding in the Holy Scriptures. When delivering the word of God, it will come out with such a might and power that burning will be in the hearts of those who hear the Word. *"Were not our hearts burning within us while He was speaking to us on the road while He was explaining the scripture to us?"* (Luke 24:32)

This fire will be protection around you wherever you go. *"And the Lord opened the servant's eyes and he saw, and behold the mountain was full of horses and chariots of fire all around Elisha"* (2 Kings 6:17). God promised to be a wall of fire for Jerusalem (Zechariah 2:4). The devil fears this fire, it reminds him what is awaiting him and so he cannot pass this wall of fire. Yes, the devil fears the fire; even the dry places torment him. He cannot find rest in dry places (Matthew 12:43).

While the devil fears this fire, the children of God must love the fire. The children of Israel were afraid of God's fire. When God spoke to them from the mountain of fire, they trembled and begged Moses to speak to them instead. Moses stood between the Israelites and God; there He declared the word of the Lord to them. They were afraid because of the fire (Deuteronomy 5:5). Bride of Christ, fear God alone and keep His commandments. If you do so, you will not be afraid of the fire but will run towards the fire like Moses at the burning bush (Exodus 3:3).

"Who among us can live with the consuming fire?
Who among us can live with continual burning?
He who walks righteously and speaks with sincerity,
He who rejects unjust gain
And shakes his hands so that they hold no bribe;
He who stops his ears from hearing
about bloodshed
And shuts his eyes from looking upon evil"
(Isaiah 33:14-15).

Chapter 12: How to Catch and Live Within the Consuming Fire

S in separates people from God. Sin blinds people so they are unable to see God's holy face. We live in a world and society which has been corrupted because of sin. So many times when we are in a place where the kingdom of God is established; there is peace, love, joy and freedom. For example, you would experience these things in a spirit-filled church. Unfortunately, when you go home after the Sunday or Wednesday service, you might be subjected to neighbors who worship idols, who practice immorality or who live ungodly lives. Sin dominates in these homes and it does not stop there. Sin is not afraid to invade Christian homes, bringing its influence into everyone's lives.

In the summer, you can be sure to find dust in almost every home. It is inevitable! You can find dust in a castle, a palace, a cabin, ugly homes, beautiful homes – it does not matter. Dust somehow infiltrates everywhere. Like dust, sin creeps in everywhere, even where it is not invited. Sin will try to knock on many men's hearts. Temptation is all around us. Even those who live a righteous life are not exempt from temptations, from committing sins. This will be so as long as we are still clothed with this flesh. What do we then do since it is inevitable that temptation and sin come to us? We need to live in God's fire every single moment of our lives. Those of us who live in the holy fire are cleansed by it every single moment, every single day of our lives. The consuming fire will burn away the chaff and everything that is not pure in the believer's life.

Today, God is looking for people who are holy, humble and hungry for Him. He is probably looking for them more than they are looking for Him. And there will come a day when these seekers will find the one sought after, and then the pursuer will catch up with the Pursued and the disciple his Master. *"You will seek me and find me when you search for me with all your heart"* (Jeremiah 29:13). We must seek with our whole hearts.

In seeking God, we must be in love with Him. Love must be the motive behind everything Christians do. The seeking, the fire, the faith – they all operate only through love. God weighs the motives of the heart and these motives must be pure. For the sake of the love of God, we seek Him and seek Him earnestly above all things. The seeker is on a journey. Jesus is the way through which the seeker passes and so the seeker seeks. There is no shortcut. If we try to enter and seek by other ways and not go through the door, then we are thieves and robbers and the fire will expose our treachery to our own shame. No one can catch the fire by entering through the doors of yoga, Buddha or worldly meditation. Also no one can catch the fire by buying it with money. The only way is through Christ alone and you must be willing to pay the price by crucifying the flesh daily. Beware of strange fire. Beware of the fire from the earth and not from heaven! Beware of those who are circumcised in the flesh but not in the heart. Many would love this fire but if they are not willing to pay the price – beware. Flesh must be crucified daily. Self must be done away with. Dear seeker, do all that is in your power to be holy, humble and hungry; thereby you will live within the fire.

Be hungry: Away with sin and worthless food!

To be hungry and thirst for God plays a great role when you enter a season of seeking. It is not possible to truly seek with determination without a hunger. A holy hunger for God must be present in order to earnestly seek Him. You might be wondering how you can be hungry for God. Answer: put away the worthless food! Your hunger, your unquenchable thirst will bring forth a desire for manna and divine drink.

"As the deer pants for the water brooks, so my soul pants for You, O God. My soul thirsts for God, for the living God" (Psalm 41:1-2). In the same way that an unquenchable thirst causes you to seek for water and does not allow you to stop seeking until you find it, hunger and thirst for God will cause you to seek and desire God and His fiery presence above all things. When you seek, you will find. It is good that you have a desire for this fire and it is a good first step. The second step is to act on that desire. So act! In the natural world, someone who is thirsty does not stay home and just say how hungry or thirsty he is. He will do something. He will go buy food. He will go fetch the water.

You must develop a holy hunger for God. It could be possible that you once knew God but that you have lost the hunger for Him and the things of God! If this is the case, remove sin from your life. Sin hinders us from having interest in the things of God. Watch out and see what kind of food you are feeding your soul. Are you feeding it the word of God or of the world? Don't spoil your appetite by eating worthless food or your thirst by drinking anything less than the Divine drink. Your soul and spirit feed from the Word of God and from fellowshipping with the Lord. You therefore ought to eat only that which comes from God's hand but nothing from the hands of satan. For if you take from satan, what do you think he is going to hand you? He does not love you. He will only give you poison, torment and affliction. Though he might hand you a cup that is very well decorated on the outside, the inside will be filled with bitterness.

"Man does not live by bread alone, but man lives by everything that proceeds out of the mouth of the Lord" (Deuteronomy 8:3). Earthly food and drink are meant to take care of the temple of God but not your soul and spirit. What are you feeding your soul? Are you eating and drinking as much as you can? Don't you know that the kingdom of God is not about eating

and drinking? Child of God, give your hand a break. Were your hands given to you to only feed you, to take and receive? What is the purpose of your hands? Why did God give you hands? Let there be a balance in your life. Use your hands to give to someone else; receive and take when necessary and only from God, not from the world. You must be willing to use your hands to give more than to receive. God Himself says it is more blessed to give than to receive.

Be hungry and thirst for God and His righteousness. I remember that when I was growing up, we hosted parties of all sorts in our home. In my family it was normal to slaughter a goat or a cow many times a year. We would invite people from nearby villages and towns to join us. Many people would come to help and they cooked for half of the day, making a great feast. As children, we were told to wait until the feast was served, so as not to spoil our appetites. Sometimes, however, we would not be willing to wait and so we would eat many snacks before the meal. When it was time for dinner, we would then have no room for the good, delicious food, so we would not be able to enjoy the feast because we chose to fill up with snacks rather than the food.

It is very important that a child of God watch out what he eats! Filling ourselves with excess of movies, gossip about celebrities, novels of all kinds, partying and worldly talk takes away the hunger for God. Those worldly things drain every bit of God's anointing from your life and instead they feed your soul with that which is rotten, taking away the holy hunger. Remember, no one will maintain his life through his sins! It is in this way people find themselves not able to have intimacy with the Lord anymore, not able to shed tears when they are seeking the Lord because they are no longer broken. They cannot cry with God and they cannot laugh with Him. The worldly things they feed on do not have mercy on their soul and leave their hearts as hard as a rock. But if you will only eat true spiritual food and give away that which you receive, God's holy hunger will increase in you.

Be hungry. Feed on the word of God. Meditate on the word of God. Seek the Lord your God with all your heart, with all your strength, and with all your might and take no rest till you get hold of Him. He who finds God finds also the fire, and God (the All Consuming Fire) will fill you up and baptize you in the Holy Spirit and fire to the fullness. When this happens, you will walk in the power of God. Jesus said "You will receive power when the Holy Spirit has come upon you" (Acts 1:8).

Be holy: Die with Christ, live through Christ and only for Christ

"I have been crucified with Christ; and it is no longer I who live, but Christ lives in me; and the life which I now live in the flesh I live by faith in the Son of God, who loved me and gave Himself up for me" (Galatians 2:20).

The journey to catch the fire will take you through the mountain of fire. It is Mount Zion and it is the Mountain of the living God. From there you can enter the heavenly city. It is a holy city. The uncircumcised and the unclean cannot travel into it. "Access denied" faces those who try to enter not by the door but by some other way. To go to this city you must go through the mountain of fire.

When God descended upon Mount Sinai in fire to meet with the children of Israel, He commanded Moses saying *"You shall set bounds for the people all around, saying, 'Beware that you do not go up on the mountain or touch the border of it; whoever touches the mountain shall surely be put to death. No hand shall touch him, but he shall surely be stoned or shot through, whether beast or man, he shall not live'"* (Exodus 19:12-13). This is the mountain to which you are journeying. You see, no man or beast could touch that mountain and live. Even today, when you go to this mountain, you cannot go relying on your own righteousness. You must be full of Jesus, dead to your flesh, living through Christ.

The journey to the mountain of fire is a great journey towards the living God. This is a journey during which you seek God and find His face. The closer you get to God, the more fire you catch and the more light you radiate. As you embark on this journey, you might wonder how could a mere man approach God and live. This mighty God whose one look causes the earth to tremble, whose touch – one touch – causes the mountain to smoke; whose presence not only causes mountains to tremble but to melt like wax before the fire! How do you make it? How can you see God's face and live, for God Himself said that no man will see His face and live? To see God, you must be dead to self. Your flesh must be already crucified with Christ. God has already made a way for you through Jesus Christ. Since He made the way, you only have to allow yourself to die with Christ, to live through Christ and to live for Christ. As you set out on this journey, know that from the departure point to your destiny there will be hundreds and hundreds of deaths!

The only way we can approach a Holy God and still live is because we have Jesus in us, the One who knew no sin. When God looks at you He sees Jesus in you and that is the only way we can get to His dwelling place, Mount Zion. Though the journey to this mountain is full of testing and trials of all sorts, it is the best place to be. This mountain is untouchable. Though persecution and trials will rise up against the one who is on his way to this mountain, these things have no power to touch him because he is hidden there in Christ. So, you do not climb alone on this mountain because you walk with Christ, accompanying Him and fellowshipping with Him. All these things promote a personal holiness. In spending time with Him, you will reflect Him.

Be humble: Bow down before God yet feel uplifted

"Seek the Lord all you humble of the earth, who have carried out His ordinances; seek righteousness, seek humility." (Zephaniah 2:3)

The Bible says that Moses was a very humble man, more humble than anyone else (Numbers 12:3). Yes, he was bumble, but he was arguably also one of the greatest men of God who ever lived. The Lord would come down and speak with Moses face-to-face just as a man speaks with his friends. This is the man who spent 40 days and 40 nights in the presence of God without interruption. He was in the presence of God so much that his face shone brightly, and they had to put a veil on his face so that people would still be able to see and meet with him after he had been with the Lord. When you look at the life of Moses however, he seemed to be the servant of all. He faithfully served the children of Israel for many years. The greatest among the children of God is the servant of all. To the degree that a man serves, to that degree is he great.

Humility is a character of Christ. Jesus said that He is gentle and humble in heart. True humility is inwardly, in the heart (Colossians 4:12). Today there are only a few Christians who are walking in true humility, and that's why not many are being used like Moses. There are many who are walking in false humility and pride, which is mostly outward. Pride and false humility are the character of satan, also known as Lucifer. Those people who have false humility and pride like to show it outwardly. They will worship for a show. They will seem to pray earnestly when the pastor passes by but if he does miss the prayer meeting – they will not even pray, they will visit with each other. True humility has been stolen from the body of Christ. Let us stand up as one person and claim it back in Jesus' name.

Many Christians know that they ought to be humble and so they indeed say "Sister, we must be humble." But their actions don't match their words! Not yet! Many people tell of the wonders they have done, not the Lord. And so, it is "I" and "me". When the little "I" and "me" has become so dominant, pride has taken hold and has usurped God's place in their lives. "I did this," and "I did that," "I" and "Me" should not be dominant. Let what you have accomplished speak for you. Children of God, let us stop pointing people to us and let us point people to Jesus instead. On the other hand, we should not lower the "I" and "me" any lower than where God meant them to be. If this occurs, we run the risk of displaying false humility.

A believer who walks in true humility will bow down before God and feel uplifted. False humility will bow before other men and seek their approval. True humility will not bow before men, but before God alone. True humility does not seek the approval of men. False humility will bow down before God and feel minimized, it will seek to please men rather than God.

God wants us purified every single moment of our lives. Living in the fire purges us and purifies us and we can always abide in God Who is all Consuming Fire. It is time for Christians to not let sin accumulate in their lives, letting it pile up and waiting for Sunday to come for deliverance. God has set you free now. Walk in your freedom every single moment of your life " It was for freedom that Christ set us free, therefore keep standing firm and do not be subject again to a yoke of slavery" (Galatians 5:1). Let us be hungry. Let us be holy. Let us be humble.

Then I, justified, will behold Your face,
Awake, I am filled with the vision of You.
O Beautiful Redeemer,
Majestic in holiness,
Deep is my longing for You.
Come O Wholly Desirable,
Fill me with Your glory.

Chapter 13: Transformed In Christ's Image

Whenever people repent and turn to the Lord, there is a change that takes place in their lives. Though this change takes place instantaneously when they give their lives to Christ, holiness and transformation is a journey in response to their willingness to change and walk with God. While salvation is a free gift, we do pay a price to live holy and righteous lives. The Bible says "it was given to her to clothe herself in fine linen, bright and clean; for the fine linen is the righteous acts of the saints" (Revelation 19:8). There has to be righteous acts on your part, otherwise you will not be given the robe of righteousness.

How does someone change and be transformed into Christ's image? Some people make a "to do" list and try to do everything on the list so that they can change. Notes and reminders are seen everywhere in their prayer journals, Bibles, computer screens and many other places, so as to remember what to do and what not to do. Though this method is good for some, it is based in the law, in law there is always death. There is a better way which is by grace and faith. Faith and grace are above, way above the law. The method of a "to do" list never worked for me, no matter how hard I tried. I attempted this method for what seemed like hundreds of times and it never worked. I found myself failing the same tasks over and over again, the very same things I thought I had mastered a couple of weeks before. One day something happened and I was given a secret that has set me free and revolutionize my life. This secret is to seek God diligently.

By diligently seeking God and spending quality time with Him, you unknowingly become like Him. "But we all, with unveiled face, beholding as in a mirror the glory of the Lord, are being transformed into the same image from glory to glory, just as from the Lord, the Spirit" (2 Corinthians 3:18). I found it impossible to use my mouth to gossip after worshipping God for hours. I found it impossible to engage myself in worldly talk after spending four hours in reading and meditating upon the word of God. I found it worthless to be impatient after waiting on the Lord all day long. I found it easy to love and forgive those who hurt me after reading and meditating on Isaiah 53. I found it useless to open my mouth to justify myself after hearing the heart of God towards me and knowing that all was well between Him and me.

Does it matter what people think about you?
If God is pleased with you,
Does anything else matter?
The condemnation of men,

The words they speak,
Their ideas and opinions about you
Are declared null and void
Before God the Righteous Judge!
They fade away when God speaks of you!

Do you remember what happened when Job's friends visited him? They said words of human wisdom. But when God came down and spoke, He did not take up the thread where Eliphaz left off, nor did He carry on from where Bildad ended nor where Zophar left off. When God came down, He took over and every one of their opinions and arguments faded away.

Anyone who cannot sleep because a sister or brother betrayed them needs to get over it. If someone can make you sleepless, they control you and they are above you. Sleep very well. All is well in the Lord...always. There will be a Judas somewhere in the circle of disciples to test you, unfortunately. If they betrayed Jesus, they will betray you too. "A disciple is not above his teacher, nor a slave above his Master" (Matthew 10:24). If they betrayed and persecuted your Master, they will betray and persecute you as well. Focus not on the betrayer but on the Redeemer; as long as your relationship with Him is great, worry not about anyone or anything. So, spend time with God and obey His word! There is a tremendous transformation that takes place when you behold God.

Prayer: Vocal

It is in seeking Him that you are in the light of His presence. The power of sin and darkness cannot hide in the light of His presence, but it is exposed and thus flees. What do I mean by seeking the Lord? I mean to take leave of everything that is a distraction and spend time with God in prayer, in worshipping and praising Him, in reading and meditating on His word, in watching with the Lord and waiting for Him in silence – soaking in His presence and gazing upon His holy face. All of these actions help to consecrate and sanctify you, for without sanctification, no one will see God. As you get closer to God, He draws closer to you. His Holy Fire starts hovering over you, cleansing and purifying you.

Prayer is about connecting one's heart to God's, arousing oneself and getting hold of Him (Isaiah 64:7). It is about coming into a loving fellowship with the Father and getting to know Him. It is about communing with the Father. Less time should be spent in asking favors and more time in finding Him and getting to know Him. He who seeks the Kingdom of God and His righteousness will be followed by all things including material and spiritual riches. God marvels at the prayer of His children who know Him because they are void of doubts and distrust but are full of a rock-like faith and trust like that of the centurion in Matthew 8:10. When you spend time in God's presence (as much time as you can), you will get to know Him. The more you know Him, the more faith you have toward Him. "And those who know your name will put their trust in you, for you O Lord have not forsaken those who seek You" (Psalm 9:10).

True prayer must be selfless. It is not about using God. It is not about seeking His hand only but it is about seeking His face, his hand and all of Him. It is not about begging either. Rather, begging shows a lack of faith. What would we say about a child whose loving father is a rich king of a mighty nation but his child is wondering how he would pay his rent and utilities? In ignorance the child goes and begs the father to please give him some money to pay rent and utilities. The father loves the child so much that he will not refuse him anything that will benefit him, plus the father owns millions of homes and buildings and has already paid for all things for this child. The begging was not because the father needed to be begged but rather because the child did not know who his father was. But once the child knows the father and his rights as a child, he simply makes a request and every need is supplied. Take time to know the Father, above all things, and secondly to know your identity in Jesus Christ.

As you pray audibly, seek to please the Father. Take time to invite the Holy Spirit to be in the room with you and fellowship with Him. Take time to worship the Father. Take time to thank Him. There is always something to be thankful for. Take time to dance for Him, remember that you are His child and He remains the Father. Pour out your heart to Him in spirit and in truth – giving all glory to Him. It is not a good idea to rush from His presence. Rushing from someone's presence means you have something else that is more important to do. ("I've got to go!") Seeking His presence is not about making fitful visits because no one should rush in the presence of a loved one. You have to understand that God is more than the best lover or friend there is, more than a visit you can receive from a President or a King of any nation. If you are not ready to give up all things and anything there is in this world for God, then you are not fit for the kingdom of God. So take time to visit with Him, let nothing rush you from out of His presence. The Holy Spirit will lead you if you let Him and you will know when it is time to wrap things up. Prayer should always end in praise, a shout of victory. You must be satisfied and very happy before you close your prayer. So pray until satisfied and filled, until you are full of joy and no longer harbor any doubt or confusion.

How long should you pray and wait in the presence of God? There is no rule about that. Let Jesus' lifestyle be your lifestyle of prayer. Study His life and you will see that it was normal for Him to spend a whole night on a mountain in prayer. King David said *"for You I wait all the day" (Psalm 25:5);* and when he had waited patiently and expectantly the Lord showed up. *"I waited patiently for the Lord; and He inclined to me and heard my cry"* (Psalm 40:1). When I got saved I used to pray maybe one hour a day or less but we had a church service every single day. I made a habit of doing this daily. There came a day however when I was more drawn into prayer, and finding the benefits of spending more time in prayer, I cried and said "Oh, my Lord, how they have lied to us! Praying longer is better!"

Who told you that you should only pray once a week? Who told you that you should only pray 15 minutes a day? Alas my friend, wake up and ask yourself who told you to do so! Certainly not the Holy Spirit! Who is the husband who is going to spend 15 minutes with his wife a day and expect a great relationship in marriage? What you sow is what you will reap. Spend little time in prayer and yield a small relationship with God. Spend much time in prayer and yield a greater intimacy with the Lord. God requires the first fruits in everything including time, not the leftovers.

Some people barely pray at all. When you ask them if they pray, their answers would be that they pray 24 hours a day for the Bible says that we ought to pray always. That's very good, but many people are just thinking and not praying, their lack of power shows that they don't pray. Prayer is not thinking! I would wish that we Christians would cease to merely think and only think about the word of God – thinking other things is harming ourselves! Another deception I have found in the ministry of prayer is that many men believe prayer is only for women. Men of God, wake up and pray! Praying makes you ready to serve God. A life without prayer makes you cold. Without prayer, there is no fire.

Prayer must be guided by the Holy Spirit. There has to be a praying in the spirit. For we as mere mortals don't know how to pray but "In the same way the spirit also helps our weakness; for we don't know how to pray as we should, but the spirit Himself intercedes for us with groaning too deep for words; and He who searches the hearts knows what the mind of the spirit is, because He intercedes for the saints according to the will of God" (Romans 8:26-27).

Prayer: Contemplative or silent

"My soul waits in silence for God only; from Him is my salvation" Psalm 63.

Bride of Christ, you have not prayed until you pray the silent prayer! Prayer is about communing with the Father. It is a two way communication. In silence, God will speak to you and you will learn to commune with Him, heart to heart. Silence is a voice too. In fact, it is such a powerful voice that it is master over noise or any other sounds.

Both a vocal prayer and silent prayer are needed. They are both very powerful. In prayer, you can both be Mary and Martha. They both are necessary. Most of the times as you pray aloud, you might be like the one working hard, fighting a spiritual battle. We can call this the "Martha prayer." There ought to be a time, however, when you cease from all works and pray the "Mary prayer." This is a contemplative prayer, done in silence – you cease from all activities and all works. This is necessary because God's work in you will not start until you stop your own works. When your words come to an end, when the tongues and the shouts come to an end, retire into your heart for He is there (John 14:17, 20). Many have missed Him because they have looked somewhere else, leaving

Him where He really is: in them. Look within for your Redeemer and you will find Him.

> *Without, evil and darkness lurks*
> *Within, light is born*
> *Without is the temporal*
> *Within is the everlasting, the eternal*
> *Without is uproar and noise*
> *Within you will find peace*
> *Without is death*
> *But within you can find Life*
> *Source of all sources*
> *Life of all lives*

Without are the things seen, the temporal things. Within however, the Eternal One lives and reigns. Within, there in your heart abide in Him. There within, it is no longer you who lives but Christ lives and you live through Him. Jesus said that when you pray you must go into your inner room. This is in your heart, into your innermost being...into the depths of your heart. There you need not speak because the possibility of becoming one with Him can become a reality.

> *In you, O Father, let me live*
> *Oh! God, my God*
> *In my heart be!*
> *There is no far,*
> *There is no near,*
> *For You and I have become one.*

There, within, it is no longer about seeking. He who seeks is the one who has not yet found. There is an intimacy that you find as you are drawn into the King's chambers. In the chamber you can become one with Him. No need to speak, no need to ask – you become one with Him. During this time of silence, it is not time to merely think, you should unite every thought with God. Every meditation must remain united with His word and all that is about Him. Do not let your thoughts shift to other matters.

In silence you will leave the outer court. You will pass by the inner court and there you will make your way into the Holy of Holies. Here God dwells. Silent in silence you receive healing, peace, knowledge, wisdom, strength and power beyond description. Heart to heart you commune with your Father. Here you give Him a chance to touch you and talk to you. In silence, one on one with the Father, you commune with Him. Mysteries are made known to you. Revelation is given. Extreme spiritual perception is born – in silence. In silence, you give God a chance to infuse His power in you. This power is imparted into you in silence and you might not even know when it occurs. But at the right time you will awake in its manifestation.

The deceiver works very well during uproar, noise and wars. But in silence he is confused. The deceiver can hide in the crowds, in the uproar, but in silence he is exposed and cannot hide. There is power in silence. It cannot be twisted, it cannot be denied, it cannot be silenced – it is a supernatural power. Silence is master over noise. Noise can be

stopped only by silence. Silence is always. Silence is very powerful! During the siege of Jericho, the walls fell down. What caused those walls to fall?
a) Faith
b) Obedience to the word of God, precepts upon precepts
c) Silence
d) Shout

Silence was one of the tools they used to cause those walls to crumble.

It would be good if people could be silent! Not only would they hear God, but they would also hear rocks, mountains and nature preach to them of the greatness of God. The world is so busy today distracting people. And the devil enjoys distracting them, keeping them busy – always doing something except the one thing that is needed: accepting Christ. They wake up in the morning and they rush to work without even giving thought to God. As they drive, they are distracted by worldly music and cell phones. At work they are under lots of pressure to meet dead lines. During lunch and breaks it is time to call family and friends and read the daily newspaper. On the way back from work they are on cell phones as they drive. Once home, they watch TV until they are tired and there is no time left for God. If people don't have time with God now, where will they spend eternity? Not with God!

Many people have no time to even pause and be silent or to ask themselves about where they will spend eternity. No wonder many people take the wide gate to destruction. They enter through it without asking for wisdom, without seeking the Lord. "For the gate is wide and the way is broad that leads to destruction, and there are many who enter through it" (Matthew 7:13). You see that they enter through it. They do not seek, they just go. "For the gate is small and the way is narrow that leads to life and there are few who find it" (Matthew 7:13). Few are those who find the narrow way and enter through it. The faithful few who do enter take time to look, seek, search and inquire. That's why the Scriptures say that they find it.

To wait for God in silence might seem hard and meaningless to the beginner but the Holy Spirit helps you as you make up your mind to do it. God's grace sees you through it. The first time when I tried to pray this kind of prayer I could not go more than five minutes. First of all, when I started doing it, within three minutes I already found myself thinking instead of praying. I could not endure and so I gave up on this kind of prayer.

Two years later I found there was something missing in my prayer life. The Holy Spirit reminded me again the contemplative prayer. Little by little, I determined to do it, and so it happened, but only for a short period of time. Day by day the Holy Spirit encouraged me and each day I made up my mind to go longer, little by little. It worked! Within 3 months of praying this kind of prayer, I attended a prayer retreat lead by Ann Goll and it was then I noticed that my spiritual life was changing tremendously. As this woman of God started sharing about the contemplative prayer, the accumulated power received during that time I spent with God – which seemed to have been dormant – was instantly and suddenly shaken and aroused in me. It was as if someone struck a match, ignited me and set me on fire. That night I had 5 different dreams from the Father!

This contemplative prayer led me into a deep understanding of the things of God. For example, after praying this kind of prayer for about three months, I could understand the Holy Scriptures that I was not able to understand before; the books that I have put on the shelves because they were too hard to understand, I could read them and gain understanding without any difficulties. Discernment and ability to understand increased in an unusual manner. I saw great results in the ministry everywhere I went. God's words became unveiled in a far greater way; many sealed things became open books!

Dreams increased in my life following the discipline of silent prayer. I asked the Lord why He spoke to me in dreams, and the Holy Spirit simply let me know that it was because in my sleep there was selah – a being still. He was able to teach me many truths and give me many revelations if I learned to selah – to be silent, to pause and be still.

Waiting for God in silence

Bride of Christ, you who longs to be with the Lord, your Lover, why do you send Him away by busying yourself with that which is not important? Watch and wait on the Lord. "The Lord is good to those who wait for Him, to the person who seeks Him. It is good that he waits silently for the salvation of the Lord" (Lamentations 3:25-26).

Tarry in the presence of God. Rush not, for he who rushes gets nowhere. In John 20, we see the disciples and Mary at the tomb. When they first came there, they did not see the Lord Jesus. They entered the tomb, not finding Jesus there they believed "they have taken away the Lord out of the tomb, and we do not know where they have laid Him." In rushing, they believed the wrong report. In rushing, all they saw was an empty tomb. However, one person made up her mind to linger in the presence of the Lord. It was Mary. By lingering and waiting for the Lord, Mary gained understanding while the other disciples in their impatience and ignorance went back to their homes believing the lies. They went home worried, hopeless and believing the wrong report. As Mary waited however, not only did she encounter angels but she also saw Jesus! She became the one who announced the good news while those who did not wait became carriers of bad news. As you linger into the presence of God, you will gain understanding, truth and revelations hidden to others who cannot wait for the Lord. You will always be the carrier of good news. Wait for your Lord.

We have waited for You eagerly
Your name
Even Your memory
Is the desire of our souls.
At night my soul longs for you

Indeed, my spirit within me seeks you
diligently
(Isaiah 26:8-9)

Blessed are those who long for God. To these, He will no longer hide Himself but their eyes will behold Him. Behold Jesus. Gaze upon Him! The more you behold Him, the more you become like Him, a mirror through which many will come to see Jesus reflected in you. How much of Jesus do you have in you? When people look at you, do they see Jesus wholly reflected or do they see the cracks in the mirror and Jesus' appearance disfigured? Anything that blocks you from reflecting Jesus blocks the way to Mount Zion for you. You are to mirror Jesus. Be pure mirrors, for only then can God reflect Himself in you. If the mirror has cracks, it will reflect crooked, imperfect pictures and you will not bring glory to the name of the Lord. Remove the cracks from the mirror by living a holy life and Jesus will be reflected in you and through you.

Watch and wait for the Lord expectantly. Wait for the God of your salvation. As you wait on Him, let Him be your only focus. You can use this time to meditate on the scriptures, or listen to beautiful worship, or just sit in His presence and love on Him. Guard your heart. Let nothing unholy enter in. If nothing unholy enters in your heart, nothing unholy will come out of it, but only that which is holy. For "Who may ascend into the hill of the Lord? Who may stand in His holy place? He who has clean hands and a pure heart..." (Psalm 24:3-4). As you start seeking God in this manner, you are ascending into God's holy mountain. You are in the secret place of the Most High as described in Psalm 91. In the secret place of the Most High, His secrets will be revealed to you. The promise in Psalm 91 is made to those who dwell in the secret place not to those who make fitful visits. There must be a quality time for communion with God.

The Puzzle
As you look unto the Lord
Mysteries are revealed
Every piece of the puzzle fall into its place
Every missing piece is given
That's the way to have the whole picture
By looking at "Him" who is the
mystery revealer

Abiding in Him

Always be conscious of God's presence. When you move, always be aware of His nearness. Praying, seeking, waiting – all must be done in God's presence. It is not about praying, worship, reading His Word first and seeking His presence but about praying, worshipping and reading in His presence. It is possible to pray His word and be far from God's presence. It is possible to worship and be far from Him for He said "In vain do they worship me" (Matthew 15:9). It is possible to read His word and be far from Him. It is possible to draw near with words and it is possible to honor Him with lip service. All must be done in His presence. Your heart of hearts must be near Him and, if possible, be one with Him.

In Him, remain
In Him, abide
In Him, live
In Him, move
Link your soul to His and allow yourself to
be united to God.

Those who dwell in the presence of the Lord will minister to Him the desires of His heart. They will be called His ministers, and He will make them a flame of fire (Hebrews 1:7). Dwelling in the presence of the Lord renders you invisible from your enemies who want to harm you. To avoid trouble, live and dwell in God's presence. To venture to go out of His presence means to expose yourself to the enemy. When you have no peace, when you are in distress, depression and despair, check your position and you will find that you went out of God's presence. God's presence never leaves those who are His, for He Himself said "I will never desert you, nor will I ever forsake you." You can, however – even though unknowingly – choose to leave His presence by giving attention to the problems of life rather than to the Answer. Remember what He said "outside are the dogs and the sorcerers and the immoral persons and the murderers and the idolaters, and everyone who loves and practices lying" (Revelation 22:15). It is better to never leave God's presence, but if you ever find yourself in depression and fear, you have moved away and you must come back into His presence.

Live in God. Every move and everything you do – do all in His presence. Abide in Him. Live in that fire. This is the fire of God's holiness and purity. This is the fire of God's love and zeal.

Where else can I find rest but in You?
Outside Your shelter,
Defenseless and unprotected am I.
Every moment I need your grace,
To abide in You,
To live in Your Love,
To dwell in Your courts,
There You enclose me behind and before.
Only there will I fear no evil!

Chapter 14: Clothed With Power from On High

"And behold, I am sending the promise of My Father upon you; but you are to stay in the city until you are clothed with power from on high" (Luke 24:49).

Unlike men, God is faithful to His promise. God is faithful in His covenant. What God promises shall come to pass regardless, for *"He who promised is faithful"* (Hebrew 10:23). God has never failed to fulfill one promise nor one word He spoke to any person. Jesus is the same yesterday, today and forever! The same promise of the Holy Spirit baptism to Jesus' disciples remains true today and forever.

Before His ascension, Jesus commissioned His disciples to go and make disciples of all the nations. True disciples give birth to disciples and this is the reason we see that Jesus still has His disciples on this planet today who are doing His work. The same words and commandments Jesus spoke to the disciples of old, He still speaks to you and to me because we are His disciples. The promise of the Father upon the disciples is the promise of the Holy Spirit; a promise of power from on high. It is written *"For the promise is for you and your children and for all who are far off, as many as the Lord our God will call to Himself"* (Acts 2:39).

"But you will be baptized with the Holy Spirit not many days from now" (Acts 1:5). This is one of the last verses Jesus spoke before His ascension, the last yet one of the most important and greatest promises. This last promise was the first to be fulfilled. How true that the last shall be the first! In order to receive this promise, however, disciples had to obey the Lord's command and be in the right place and position to receive. Jesus commanded the disciples not to leave Jerusalem but to tarry and wait for the Holy Spirit. As they observed all He commanded them to do, not only did they receive the Holy Spirit but they also received the fire, for the tongues of fire came and distributed and rested on each one of those who obeyed the Lord's command. All Jesus' disciples throughout the ages are commanded to observe all things Christ commanded the early disciples. Today, this command still remains "Wait for what the Father has promised: The Holy Spirit and the fire. Do not leave Jerusalem till you are clothed with the power from above." In order to have an effective ministry like that of the early apostles, we must be clothed with power from on high. We must also be baptized in the Holy Spirit and fire. He who serves without this

baptism can be compared to a man at the battlefield who does not have his weapons or ammunitions.

Armed with Divine weapons of mass destruction

God does not send any disciples to work for Him without first equipping them. The commander does not send his army out without giving them weapons, ammunitions, provision and anything they will need for the battle. Jesus did not say they should be witnesses first and receive the power afterward – oh no! They had to wait first and be clothed from on high and then they could be witnesses. The scriptures clearly say *"But you will receive power when the Holy Spirit has come upon you; and you shall be my witnesses both in Jerusalem, and in all Judea and Samaria and even to the remotest part of the earth."* (Acts 1:8). Jesus did not send the disciples to witness and then receive power afterwards. It is power first and then service, for this is the power for service, the supernatural power to serve God with signs and wonders confirming that His word is alive and true. Even when Jesus sent the 12 and then the 70 disciples out, He gave them power and authority first and then He sent them out. This is the power upon which the church is built (Matthew 16:18). Alas, today you can easily find many people who are trying to serve Him even though they have been dressed upside down! They have made it service first and then power. Is the church going forward or backward? The church should go forward. From glory to glory the church must go.

Lord, I pray that You would Unveil the eyes of the ones trying to serve you today without the power from on high. They have done all they can but they barely see any victory. They are having little results and do not see fruits. Their intentions are good but something is missing! Where are the remaining fruits? Oh, Lord help! Many shepherds are weak and weary; they don't know what to do! As shepherds, they have worked so hard raising many sheep, but Lord...today they cannot recognize their sheep anymore for some have become weak clay vessels, other have turned into wolves, others have become ungodly and are practicing homosexuality using Your name! Others are proclaiming their selfishness as pro-choice, not allowing their precious babies to have a choice. They deny the truth in the womb. These shepherds toil from their flesh and so flesh gives birth to flesh; miserable weak vessels are born. Thus they give birth to weak Christians who cannot please God for it is written that those who are in the flesh cannot please God. Every shepherd must have this power from on high. If they have it they will affect millions; no, billions of lives! If they don't have this power from on high however, they will see billions of lives going to hell because they neglected the power of God.

Be prayerful, be upright in your heart and weapons of mass destruction will be given to you. The prayer of the righteous avails much. Shepherds and their sheep, like soldiers, must be equipped with weapons of power of mass destruction before they go to war. It is a must that they keep the weapons in their hands and their armor on, lest they become prey to the evil one. The enemy of the Gospel, satan, knows those who are equipped with the weapons of mass destruction, and he also knows those who go to war without weapons. Though they can hide it from people, they cannot hide it from satan who is attacking them. True, satan knows who you are. We see demons telling Jesus *"We know who you are"*; demons know what your task is, so you had better do it right. We see them saying to Jesus *"What business do we have with each other, Jesus of Nazareth? Have you come to destroy us?"* (Mark 1:24). They knew Jesus' task very well, for the scriptures say that *"The son of God appeared for this purpose, to destroy the works of the devil"* (1 John 3:8). So the devil knows your task and he knows whether or not you are clothed with power from on high.

Hot for Jesus

Jesus said *"But if I go I will send Him to you"* (John 16:7.) The Holy Ghost has been sent to you and to your church. Receive Him; don't shut Him outside the door of your heart and your church. Don't put out the fire. *"Do not put out the Spirit's fire"* NIV (1 Thessalonians 5:19). You can receive Him now – the disciples received Him, I received Him and many saints have received Him. Only believe. All things are possible to them that believe. Ask God to baptize you in the Holy Spirit – be completely immersed in Him and don't stop there. Go deeper and receive the baptism of the fire. For as the Holy Spirit fell upon the 120 in the upper room, tongues of fire were distributed on each one of them and they received the baptism of fire at the same time. With the coming of this baptism of the Holy Spirit and the fire, miracles of all sorts took place. Read the book of Acts, dig deeper and you will be amazed at what many Christians and churches are missing out today. There are some churches that are walking in this power, praise God. Let every church that is called by the name of the Lord walk in this power, Amen.

You might say that you already have been commissioned to do the work by the Lord and so you don't think you need this fire. Read the scriptures and you will find that Jesus' disciples had received power years before, yet Jesus told them to wait for the baptism of the Holy Spirit and the fire. They even had some gifts, yet after His death and resurrection, we see Jesus commanding them to wait for what the Father had promised and not to leave Jerusalem until they were filled with the power from on high. Why? Because though they had received power, they had not yet received the baptism of the Holy Spirit and fire, they had not been immersed and buried in this baptism. Yes, they needed to receive the Spirit and the fire before starting their ministry, before becoming apostles, before shaking the whole world with the True Gospel. This baptism is the fullness of God in the believer's life and as you can tell following what took place after they were filled, they turned many people to righteousness setting them on fire for God wherever they went. It is God's desire that all His disciples be filled to the fullness of God.

Be dunked in this river of God's fire, be immersed in it and be full of fire and bring a fire invasion wherever you are sent. It is important to be on fire. The people who are neither hot nor cold will be spit out of God's mouth! *"So because you are lukewarm, and neither hot nor cold, I will spit you out of My mouth"* (Revelation 3:16). The things that are keeping some of you from being hot; the pleasures of this world that are preventing you from abandoning yourselves wholly to God will be the first to mock on the day when the lukewarm are spewed out of God's mouth. How terrible will be that day for them that have put this word off for tomorrow! Without the fire no one can be hot. Choose today whether you will be lukewarm, cold, or hot! I trust God that we are all going to vote for hot! Let us all become hot for Jesus. How many cold hearts are you going to warm? See the joy there is in bringing warmth to a cold heart. Once you sow this seed, it only multiplies because it is eternal! It never dies, it only multiplies! Praise the Holy One of Israel Who clothes us from on high. We will in reality set the world aflame, and all to the glory of our God!

The fire of judgment

But for the disobedient and rebellious, the fire of God brings judgment (Isaiah 66:15.)

While the children of God love the fire, the wicked and the enemies of God hate this fire. The fire of God slew the men who carried up Shadrach, Meshach and Abednego. The guards who made this fire were the very ones who were destroyed by it. The fire they made by their own hands killed but only them. The trap of the evil one thus slew those that set it up. The wicked fell into their own nets, while the righteous passed by safely. Why? The fire of God burns everything that is impure, everything that is not purely from God must be burned at the coming of this fire. These guards were for sure full of wickedness and impurity, and nothing could pass through the fire in them and come out as gold, so they burned. This fire burns to dust all that is dead, all that is evil. Since the wicked are full of evil, when they pass through the fire they will burn. However, those who were pleasing to God passed through the fire refined.

The book of Malachi, chapter 4 talks about the day of the Lord that is coming. That day is burning like a furnace. Though this day is terrible and full of fire, the children of God rejoice at its coming because God promises them "But for you who fear My name, the sun of righteousness will rise with healing in its wings; and you will go forth and skip about like calves from the stall. You will tread down the wicked for they will be ashes under the soles of your feet on the day which I am preparing." But though this day is exciting to the righteous, see what it says about the unrighteous: "All the arrogant and every evil doer will be chaff; and the day that is coming will set them ablaze."

Demons don't like for people to talk about this fire. They don't want any preacher to preach this message of fire. The very mention of this fire causes them to tremble. They are so scared about this fire that they are even scared by dry places (Luke 11:2.) They cannot stand any dry places; they cannot find rest in the waterless places. The dry and waterless catches fire easily, so demons are scared about even a dry place! The fire of God goes before Him and devours and burns up His enemies round about (Psalm 97:3).

When God brought judgment upon Sodom and Gomorrah, He rained brimstone, sulfur, and fire out of heaven upon the city. The city and all its inhabitants and everything in it was overthrown because of the wickedness of the people in the land. While the fire is good to God's children, to the wicked and disobedient, this fire is judgment.

A revolutionary cry: Set me on heavenly fire

Alas, our God! Your altar has been ready all along. You have waited for us for so long. We have put you on hold for too long, wandering around aimlessly, trying to act on Your behalf within our own power. We have burned out trying to serve because we leaned on our own understanding but today we say: "Enough is enough". So we send a revolutionary cry to You! We want the Holy Spirit, we desire Your fire, we want Your power, we can no longer serve in our own strength. Here at your altar we offer ourselves up to You. Receive the sacrifice. Take over our lives and be in our hearts!

Bride of Christ, go through the preparation and embark on a journey to catch the fire. Do not fix your eyes on how long it will take. Rather, fix your eyes on Jesus who baptizes with the Holy Spirit and the fire. Do not let the time be an issue for you. You are beyond time because you are eternal. Empty your vessel and come forward. An empty vessel will be filled. He will indeed fill you with fire. Freely walk the highway of holiness. Freely be burned, cleansed and purged by His holy fire. Do not be afraid of the fire for it is given to you for your benefit and the benefit of God's kingdom. It will only burn the chaff, the perishable, the temporal and the no-longer-good that keeps the light and the glory of God from being seen through you. Desire the fire! Love the fire!

Allow complete burning

You are a child of God. And so on this journey through the mountain of holy fire you go. Allow yourself to be touched and completely burned by God's refining fire. Allow a complete burning. Do not come out of the furnace of fire until all bondages are burned and you are free indeed. Do not come out until you are loosed. Beware of the false fire, the strange fire. Beware of false burning. God's true fire is a heavenly fire. God's true fire burns up the chaff in believers' lives. True fire ignites the new heart to become a living flame of love for God. Incomplete burning will have nothing rising up but smoke and the sacrifice will only include the no-longer-good. Let the fire burn away all that will not pass through as gold; for gold is refined by the fire. Let this fire consume you whole, only then will you be the heavenly fire carrier.

Living in the consuming fire of God, you cannot be destroyed by it. At the burning bush, Moses was not destroyed by the fire and he did not run from it, but he ran toward the fire. As he turned towards the fire, he heard the voice of God calling Him (Exodus 3:3-4). Shadrach, Meshach and Abednego were not destroyed by it but were loosed and walked in the fire with God, free indeed. When you turn toward the fire, when you live in the fire, only that which is not pure will be destroyed. This fire cleanses you, purging and purifying you. While the incomplete burning will be but smoke and mist, never rising above, true burning will be a pure flame ascending high above you bringing warmth and joy to all. This is a new journey, a new level, a beautiful and awesome never-ending transformation.

New vessel of fire

In the fire, you are made brand new. In the fire, you will be given a brand new mouth that will utter those words which are only holy. When you come towards God, the Eternal Fire, the burning coals in the seraphim's hands will touch your mouth. "Behold, this has touched your lips, and your iniquity is taken away and your sin is forgiven" (Isaiah 6:6-7).

Let the tongues of fire touch you. Tongues of fire will rest upon you till you are filled with the fullness of God. These tongues of fire will cause new tongues to be born in you. Like the 120 in the upper room, you will speak the new tongues. The new tongues will cause new ears to be born to hear anew.

When you are touched by this holy fire, the light of God will unveil your eyes. New eyes will be given to you with the purpose of shining so that all who you meet will be touched by the light of God's presence. Let the new light in your eyes shine and only see the new things God is doing.

And yes, in the fire you will receive new hands! Let new hands grow in your hands to receive from heaven and give forth that which is from heaven. New hands that will not hold but give and give and give from God.

Oh, the greatness of God! With God, and the fullness of God in you, all things become new: new taste, new hearing, new sight, new touch, new smell. Cast the old away; let all be done with the new ear, new mouth, new tongues, new eyes, new hands...let all be done by the newness.

Once you are baptized with the Holy Fire, you become a new vessel. Make sure the only thing in the vessel is this blazing holy fire. He who is from below can baptize you with water, but only He who is from above can baptize with the fire, for He is above all. Be therefore filled with the fire, let go of everything else in the vessel that is not from above.

Now that you have the heavenly fire

Now that you have the fire of God, keep it at all costs. There is nothing such as "I have arrived". You will not arrive until you cross through the gates into the everlasting Beautiful City – your heavenly eternal home. But before then, there has to be a daily striving, there has to be a daily price to pay! Living and walking daily in the heavenly fire you will radiate tongues of fire. Fire invasion will touch other people through you but you must act. No one will catch it; nothing will happen if you don't act. Act and pass the fire on. Give it to all without judgment. God lets His sun shine on the righteous as well as on sinners. May this be a good reminder to you, give the fire to everyone without judging. This is a fire of love. Give it in love. Without love, nothing can be. There is no flame, no fire without love! Pass it on then in love. Bring transformation everywhere you go. The holy fire in you will cause many people who come near to be hot and catch the fire, just as we are warmed by the fire when we come near it.

Bride of Christ, how wonderful it is to be baptized in the holy fire. It is an extraordinary level but one that requires extraordinary work and discipline. There are many things you will have to leave behind in order to live, move and walk in God's holy blazing fire. There are many things that will need to be cut off from your life.

Pass on the fire: This blazing holy fire you receive, you will keep it only by giving it away. In the physical realm, this does not make sense – you want to keep something and the requirements are to give it away? Yes, that's how things work in the kingdom of God. Do you want to be blessed? Be a blessing to others first. Do you want to receive? Then first give! Things in the kingdom of God work exactly the opposite of this world's system. You cannot keep this holy fire by holding on to it. You keep it by giving it away. In giving you receive it back, only multiplied. Always giving it, always receiving it, and always having more than you gave. The fire must not be put out but must be passed on. The more fire you pass on, the more fire you receive. The secret of multiplication for this fire is in giving it out, passing it on!

Remove stumbling blocks: Stumbling blocks must be removed when they come into your path. Do not resort to self-pity, no matter how these things might seem dear to you. It is good to have two hands or two feet, but if one of them causes you to stumble, you must cut it off. Anything in you that is not serving God, anything in you that keeps you from staying on the path of life, cut it off, roots and fruits. Cut it off, all of it. It is better for you to enter eternal life with one foot, with one hand rather than having two and be cast into the fiery hell.

Get rid of sin: Do not defend sin in you and do not side with sin. Don't tolerate it. Even if it hurts, you must ask for the sword and you must cut it off in Jesus' name. Do not fear cutting away the dead roots and fruits. The apple that is rotten must be removed from the rest no matter how good it smells. If they all stay in one basket, they will all start to rot because of the one that is bad. The branch that is dead or does not bring fruits must be removed and taken away from the tree. A new bud will grow in its place.

Take care of the fire: Bride of Christ, nourish and take care of the fire you receive. *"Do not put out the Spirit's fire"* NIV (1 Thessalonians 5:19). The fire must be kept. Praise God for the Holy Spirit, your Highest Helper. You will keep the fire not by might nor by power but by the Spirit of the Living God. His rushing wind will blow the fire when you allow Him to. Remember to fellowship together with your brothers and sisters in Christ, the fire carriers – it is a glorious and wonderful thing. The burning coal that remains standing by itself cannot keep the fire. But burning coals together bring a powerful and unquenchable fire. When fire carriers come together, the combined fire burns hotter. And burning flames bring more light.

Like the early apostles, read, study and devote yourself to the teaching of the word. Stay in the fellowship with the body of Christ. Worship God and pray without ceasing. Walk with God and seek His Holy Face continually. Be in His presence and abide in Him.

In the midst of heavy storms,
When the floods lifted up their pounding waves,
You commanded the storms "be still"
You hushed the waves of the sea!
O – Rock of my salvation,
Whilst persecuted, forsaken, betrayed and mocked;
You have kept me in perfect peace!
In the depth of Sheol,
I cried to You for help,
You rescued me from the night monsters;
You preserved my heart from sinning against You.
O Tower of Strength against my enemies!
Your love sustained me,
Your power and grace lifted me up,
In your shelter I found true refuge!

Chapter 15: Fire of Testing and Persecution

"We went through fire and through water, yet you brought us out into a place of abundance" (Psalm 66:12).

Now that you are full of fire, you are very dangerous to the enemies of God. You are on the frontline in the army of the Most High, whose commander is God Almighty. Within you are great weapons of mass destruction. The enemies of God know what a threat you are to the kingdom of darkness and so wish for harm. They will do all they can to cause you to sin and lose your weapons. They will try to force you to give up, but take courage; the battle you are in has already been won. Satan will use fear, intimidation, misunderstanding, slander, persecution and other evil weapons against you, to discourage you in your upward climb. Do not fear tribulations or death. Death and Hades hover over the earth seeking whom to kill, but fear not. Jesus, your friend, holds the keys of Hades and death (Revelation 1:18).

Why persecution?

The higher the mountain you climb, the fewer things you can take along! What if you have to go through water or fire? Is there anything to take along? I tell you, there is nothing but life itself! Nothing! You will be stripped of many things – they are all temporal things, however. But as you first seek God and His kingdom, all these things will follow you and also persecutions (Mark 10:30). So losing things should not be an issue for all these things will follow you when you leave all for His sake.

"A disciple is not above his teacher, nor a slave above his Master" (Matthew 10:24). If Jesus was persecuted, then His disciples will be persecuted also. The greater the fire you carry, the greater the persecution you will suffer. Look at the life of David, Elijah; look at the life Jeremiah, John the Baptist and other true prophets of God. Look at Jesus, Your Savior! They all went through a great time of testing and trials.

The baptism of fire comes with great persecution. It is a persecution to the first degree! The moment you receive the mantle of fire, you are enlisted on the most wanted list in the kingdom of darkness. Look at the life of the disciples before and after the day of Pentecost. Before the baptism of fire, life was very good for them. If anyone had to suffer persecution, it was Jesus! Immediately after receiving the baptism of the Holy Spirit and the fire however, things were changed. We see Peter and John being arrested; James was put to death by Herod; Stephen was stoned to death; Paul and Silas were imprisoned and persecution increased against all the believers. We see John on the island of Patmos because of persecution and more disciples were imprisoned and eventually martyred because of their faith in Jesus.

All who live godly lives in Christ Jesus will be persecuted. The soul that is wholly resigned to God will be persecuted. The trials you will go through during this time are unusual and unique, so it does not help to compare yourself to others. For the weak, persecution will be their downfall, but for the strong it will be their rise and triumph! As you hold tightly onto Jesus, you will come to know Him more and more. Once you know who your God really is, then you will find yourself renouncing all for His sake. God is so captivating, and once you fall in love with Him you will never go back. By renouncing all for His sake then, all will also renounce you. This division must occur, and it is very natural. Deny all for His sake and all will deny you. The Lover that you pursue now; He is all you need! In the same way food seems to be tasteless after eating desserts and all sorts of sweets, once you taste and see that the Lord is good, it is impossible to find comfort outside Him. When you taste the best, you leave what is not as good behind.

Fire divides

"I have come to cast fire upon the earth; and how I wish it were already kindled! But I have a baptism to undergo, and how distressed I am until it is accomplished!" (Luke 12:49)

There is something that happens once you get the fire: division occurs. It must happen. Fire divides. Wherever fire burns, true and false will be separated – it is must! Wherever fire spreads, wood and hay and stubble will burn to ashes while gold remains.

Jesus Christ preached a message of fire which pierced the hearts of the people who heard it. It was a message full of life and authority. This message of fire was not always welcomed, however. In the gospel of Luke, we read that Jesus preached a message of fire that all who heard it spoke well of Him and caused them to wonder at the gracious words falling from His lips. Since He preached such a great message, one would think that all those people would have loved Him! That was not the case. We see the same people filled with rage and driving Him out of the city, wanting to kill him. Many times, Jesus' words caused divisions in the crowds among those who were His and those who were not; *"So a division occurred in the crowd because of Him"* (John 7:43). Whenever miracles occurred in Jesus' ministry, division automatically followed. Why was there this division? Because evil and good cannot live together. Righteousness and unrighteousness can not kiss each other. These two classes must separate even on their own accord. There must be a separation between the class of good and evil.

Through the fire

When you walk through the fire, you will not be scorched,
Nor will the flame burn you" (Isaiah 43:3).

Satan will try to cause you pain and hurt so that you will be full of unforgiveness, hatred and revenge. Regardless of what is done to you (injustice, false accusations, slanders), whether small or great, yours is to keep your heart pure before your God. Regardless of what is done to you, you must love, forgive and bless them that persecute you. Allow the Holy Spirit to help you love them that persecute you, "Because the love of God has been poured out within our hearts through the Holy Spirit who was given to us" (Romans 5:5). Be full of joy. If the persecutors can take your joy away, then they have won over you. Be full of joy. Be very bold and strong. Seek no sympathy nor consolation nor approval from people. Carry everything to God in prayer.

The enemies of God will try to cause you to have sorrow and regrets. Have no sorrow, have no regrets even if you did something wrong – repent, confess your sins to God and to one another, then let go of the sorrow and regrets. Delight yourself in the Lord. He will bring justice to you at the right time. That fire which you have received, you will be tempted to give it up in many ways, but keep it at any cost. Be prepared because the battle will not be an easy one. Remember that God has equipped you to overcome. So fight, win, and overcome, you champion in the army of the Lord of Host. Yes, receiving and keeping the fire might cost you the loss of all temporal things (praise God that they are only temporal things), but take courage. Though you might go through many trials, remember that you have power to bear no burden, not even one, because God bears them for you every day! *"Blessed be the Lord, who daily bears our burdens"* (Psalm 68:19). Cast your cares therefore upon the Lord and He will sustain you. Yours is the task to remember to give all those burdens to God.

The enemy will mobilize his most evil demons and their wicked agents, and will direct them against you in a greater way. *"Do not fight with small or great, but with the king of Israel alone"* (2 Chronicles 18:30). Why? Because they know that an army without a leader is vulnerable; an army without a commander is indeed in great havoc. At no fault of your own, you will find yourself going through the hardest testing and trials. Many times you will be persecuted, forsaken, humiliated and mocked. You might be humiliated in public and before many other people. You might find yourself being made a spectacle. But fear not, all these shall come to pass. The Lord will restore your honor everywhere the enemy tried to humiliate you.

During the first time of trials, you might find yourself telling all that you are going through to friends, but I found it useless to carry your burdens to people. It is better to bring them to God. Don't expect people, friends and family to understand you and be on your side; "then all the disciples left Him and fled" (Matthew 26:56). The people who carry the heavenly fire or who will carry it later will be the only ones to understand you. But those who don't carry the fire, they will misunderstand you. They will say that you are too holy, that you have lost your mind. "When His own people heard of this, they went out to take custody of Him; for they were saying, "He has lost His senses." (Mark 3:21). They said the same to Jesus and they might say the same to you. People will leave you. Be prepared and face this with strength and love. Sometimes it will be your own people. Jesus was taunted by His own brothers. The Bible says that even His own brothers did not believe in Him (John 7:3-5). Don't be alarmed if your family and friends stand with the enemies who satan is using to take away the fire from you. Be prepared to love and forgive in advance, because many will oppose you and be convinced that you are wrong. Truly, many won't be by your side during this time. Many times, you will be left all alone! Jesus was alone when He carried the cross. The same thing will happen to you. In the same way Jesus did not retaliate nor keep revenge and unforgiveness in His heart towards Peter, who denied Him, nor anger at Judas, who betrayed Him but loved them to the very end, love them in the same way. Allow nothing in your heart but love. Do not make room for one single sin, nor unforgiveness, nor revenge in your heart. Pray for your enemies, bless those who persecute you for they don't know what they are doing.

Through the mighty waters

"When you pass through the waters, I will be with you;
And through the rivers, they will not over-flow you.
(Isaiah 43:3)

Dear reader, read this and believe it! First of all we can be certain that we are passing through the waters. In other words, we are heading to the other side. Many times when we face this battle, we can forget that it is only for a season. Remember that we are going through, and this is not the end of all things. It is only a temporal thing and it will therefore come to pass. Take courage, there are saints throughout the ages past who have gone before us. They went through these mighty waters and they made it to the other side victoriously. They did finish strong and their actions encouraged many of us to keep the faith. Through the fire and through the water...these kinds of spiritual warfare have many uncertainties, but allow God to become your certainty.

Look at Moses and the children of Israel. Moses told them that *"The Lord will fight for you while you keep silent"* (Exodus 14:14). Looking at the waters of the Red Sea, the children of Israel trembled! Any time that men look at the problems they are facing outwardly through the mortal eye, they will tremble.

But if men look at the problem they are facing inwardly through the eyes of God, the problem itself will tremble and be no more, just like that mountain which Jesus talked about: *"but even if you say to this mountain, 'Be taken up and cast into the sea', it will happen"* (Matthew 21:21). Look up to God and fear Him alone. When you fear God, there will never be any fear of man or of situations in you! Don't you know that God has the power to gather waters of the sea together as a heap? Fear no man, fear nothing, only fear God!

The step of faith

The children of Israel cried out. God said to them: *"Go forward, why are you crying out to me?"* (Exodus 14:15). Go forward, victorious prayer warrior - go forward, through the mighty waters, go forward. How? By a step of faith. You don't have to see the way in order to go forward. The way will be made by that step of faith. Go forward through these mighty waters and you will get to the other side. There is no shortcut and there is no escape. Face it and go through it! There is no way given to you. The way is made out of a step of faith you take. The step of faith helps you walk on a way-less way.

How do you walk on a pathless way? How do you walk on the mighty water like Peter? How do you cross what seems to be a great chasm to the other side. Is this possible? Yes it is – take the step of faith and remember to not look back, but look only to Him who walked on the water, Jesus Christ Your

Savior. Remember that all things are God's servants. Everything can be a way: the mighty waters are a way, the fire is a way, and persecution is a way. Only God is the creator and all things were created by Him, created by God out of nothing. Out of a void, out of a chasm, out of mighty waters, God was, and is, able to create a way. It is He who opens rivers on bare heights, who creates a pool of water in the wilderness and causes fountains of water to gush forth from dry land. Since God is a creator, if you don't see a way, relax! He will do something new and you will be taken by surprise seeing how He delivers you.

After God instructed them to go forward, the children of Israel went forward, obeying the word from God. After they obeyed, the waters divided. What had seemed deadly God used to save! Frontline warrior, if you have faith not only can you walk on water but you can also walk on nothing, on the empty space. By obeying and stepping out by faith, the water was divided in two and there was a dry ground on which to walk. There is a better way that can only be made by stepping out in faith and doing what you dread. Fear God only. Fear in other things is running to idols. Tear them down and fear God only. Dare to do what you could not do before! You see how a way was born by a step of faith, walking in a way-less way! Praise God! The water parted in two. They walked on dry ground! This dry ground could not have been made without the mighty waters. Do you see this creative miracle? In order for it to take place, there had to be the mighty waters!

Take heed! Do not be envious nor desire anything from the unbelievers. Even though God gives material blessing to believers and non-believers (His sun shines on the believers and those who don't believe), it is not so when it comes to spiritual blessings! The Bible says that when the children of disobedience walked through the waters, they drowned and the deep covered them; they went down into the depths like a stone to be found no more! Yes, there will be persecution, fire and might waters but remember that these are only taking you into a miraculous, supernatural journey with your God. Because this path is merely made out of faith, the disobedient cannot walk through it; they will drown. But you will walk through it and make it to the other side.

In Gethsemane & in death

In due season, you will move from the time of testing and trials into a time of death. You will find yourself into Gethsemane! O, Gethsemane, such a place that many dare not tread! It is a place where you are on your knees, a place where you remain and watch with the Lord as you wait for the betrayer to come and hand you over to the mob. It is a place full of grief and distress. In Gethsemane, you will ingly let your will go and embrace the perfect will of God. In Gethsemane you are stripped of your rights, even when you are oppressed and afflicted, you will not open your mouth. In Gethsemane, sleep not but watch! Prayer will keep you from temptation. Prayer will keep you moving till you overcome.

In Gethsemane, you choose God's perfect will. You accept the cup and drink it. In Gethsemane, cut all the stumbling blocks. Leave old friends behind, they cannot enter through the door you are about to enter, you must go through it alone. In Gethsemane, remove all the stumbling blocks; you will be stripped off all things and you will remain naked. "Don't bind yourself to anything." The lesson of not binding yourself to anything is a great one. Those of you who the Lord has blessed with the riches of this world, listen carefully. It is good to have those blessings. I believe they are from the Lord. However, don't bind yourself to any earthly thing and don't tie yourself to those temporal things. When you bind yourself to those things, you lose your freedom little by little. It is in this way that many people find themselves not being able to sleep at night; it is in this way people have stress; it is in this way people find themselves weighed down. How can you be weighed down when your Jesus is the Corner Stone and the Weight Bearer? He Himself said "Come to me all who are weary and heavy laden and I will give you rest" (Matthew 11:28).

In Gethsemane, pray fervently, intercede, like a mother who is about to have a baby, push hard, cry out to God fervently.

In Gethsemane, your betrayer will meet you there. Stand up and meet your betrayer. The betrayer could be anyone of the disciples, from the inner circle. The betrayer will lead the mob and they will come against you. Judas the betrayer will then give you a kiss of betrayal! The mob will lay hands on you, they will seize you. As this happens all will leave you and flee. Alone, you will be tried! Many who know you might come and be witnesses against you and false testimony against you will be given. The betrayer will have many, crowds of people on his side and many letters of recommendations for him and against you, those letters of recommendations might be written by your own sisters and brother or friends. The mob will mock you and spit you in the face, they will hurl abuse against – even some will do so without knowing you... they just follow the crowds and try to fit in the group. As this happens, many you thought were on your side will publicly deny you. You will be taken away and they will say "I do not know the man." They will deny you not once but many times.

Fear not, the truth will win. There is a purpose behind all of this. Remember, "Unless a grain of wheat falls into the earth and dies, it remains alone but if it dies, it bears much fruit." (John 12:24). O, Refiner's Fire – Your plans are beyond our comprehension! There is nothing that will happen to you at this stage without the Father's consent. You are being prepared for a resurrection power.

> *"Then all the disciples left Him and fled"*
> *"Many false witnesses came forward "*
> *"He deserves death" They said!*
> *"Crucify Him"..."Release Barabas"*
> *"I don't know the man" Peter said*
> *"Truly, this was the son of God"*

They will try you. You will be condemned. They will accuse you, but let your words be few! You owe them no explanation, God is your Advocate. The resurrection power is ahead. You will be handed over for crucifixion. The end of Judas and those who enjoy afflicting the righteous is certain. Judas will weep bitterly. The spirit of repentance having left him, he will have no peace. Those who help Judas or hire him, they will not care for him in his misery. In that world of misery they will say "what is that to us?"; "See to that yourself." (Matthew 27:4).

After being crucified with Christ, you will experience a resurrection power. It will no longer be you who live but Christ living through you. Wherever you go, the blessings of the Most High will be showered everywhere you are sent. With Christ living through you, His anointing will flow through you in a powerful way. Yes, there is a special anointing that comes with persecution.

The persecutors

Being persecuted by outsiders can be understandable, but how is it that in many instances it is the church goers, the religious leaders, the false brothers and false sisters who persecute? It could even be your own pastor! If you look in the book of Acts, you will see that the priests and even the high priests persecuted the apostles and the believers. Persecutors can be any one from any walk of life – even people who have no relationship with God and His Christ. You will know them by their lack of power. Don't be astonished that most of them have so much knowledge. They can quote the scriptures and memorize most of it. Don't be surprised about that because satan himself quoted the scriptures to Jesus! He could quote it but could not live it nor demonstrate it! In the same way, many so called Christians who persecute the children of God can in no way demonstrate the Word of God because they don't live it. They can quote it but no miracles will come to confirm what they say. You will know them by:

- Their fruits: They cannot produce fruits that remain.
- Their lack of power: They can act as though they have power but they have no real fruits.
- Reading the scriptures for the wrong reasons: Usually they read to prove to themselves how right they are and how sister or brother so-and-so is wrong. Their hearts are not right, so when they see other people, they see the wrong motives.
- Denying the power of God: They do not believe in the anointing and the power of the Holy Spirit.
- Their accusations: They are full of accusations even as their father the devil is called the accuser of the brethren.
- Their judging of others: They have pointing fingers and they judge the most anointed servants of God.
- Their lack of love: They are full of anger, mockery and void of true love.

- Seeking the glory of men: They are man pleasers and they like the approval of man rather than the approval of God.
- Contradicting: They like to contradict others and see error before they see anything good in people.
- Prideful: They take pride in being able to quote scriptures, however they do not live them.
- They live a prayerless lifestyle
- Enemies of God: They are the enemies of the Gospel of Jesus Christ, full of deceit, fraud, sons of the devil and enemies of all righteousness (Acts 13:10).

To such as these, flee from them! For *"How blessed is the man who does not walk in the counsel of the wicked, nor stand in the path of sinners, nor sit in the seat of scoffers!"* (Psalm 1:1). They have too much knowledge and they are on the devil's assignment to spiritually drain you, to bring doubts and to cause you to fall. You cannot prove anything to them for they have too much knowledge. The language you speak is a strange language to them. It is very hard for such as these to be saved. Pray for them – pray for them that persecute you for they don't know what they are doing. Do not retaliate when you are persecuted. Vengeance belongs to God. Your task is to pray for your persecutors. The eye of those who dwell in Christ should look on them with great sympathy and love. You must forgive; it is not an option!

Fight from a spiritual position

The enemy will try to cause you to give total attention to the problems rather than the answer, who is Jesus. Here is wisdom: fix your eyes on your Savior. The eye not focused on the outward is in the right place to see the new thing God is doing and it can easily detect the deceiver. The more attention you give to the problem, the bigger the problem becomes. The magnitude of a problem comes from the attention you give to that problem.

Fix your eyes upon Jesus with a permanent gaze. One look, or two, or three or even one thousand will not do it. It must be a continual and a permanent gaze. Can the mortal eye be fixed on Jesus? Not only will it be tried, but it can never behold He who is Spirit. Flesh cannot behold that which is spirit. Flesh sees flesh. But the spiritual eyes see both flesh and spirit. We therefore know that fixing your eyes upon Jesus is not a matter of doing it with physical eyes but spiritual eyes. Let then your whole heart and attention be fixed on Jesus. Determine to let go off all things. Determine to give Him access to each room of your heart. Many of you are still holding keys to your own inner rooms that you have not released to Him. Any prisoner can be free, except the self imprisoned. Give Him the keys to the rooms in your heart and let Him set you free. Let Jesus have full access in you and you will be full of Him.

When you fix your eyes on Jesus, you will get His vision. It is like putting on glasses for those who have difficulty seeing well. When you do so, you see clearly. It is not that the object you are looking at has changed; it is that your perception has changed to see the reality of what is already there. You have the glasses, put them on! Put on Jesus; see through the eyes of God.

Do you see evil? Is your mind lost on the loss of a job, relationship, money, business, marriage, a loved one or a place of honor? Have you allowed your mind to wander into the future and have you already anticipated failures? Have you become so learned that you know the future above the Almighty? Have you already decided that you will not make enough money to pay that rent and will lose that house? That it is too late? That nothing can be done? Have you already concluded that the promise God gave you will not come to pass? That your ministry is not successful and there is no way you will make it? That you will not pass the test, that you will not please so and so? Child of God, how dare you anticipate future failures. The Almighty has already decided that there is a future for you and there is hope (Jeremiah 29:11). Don't you know that a man was made by the Creator and to him he did not give the capacity to carry the load of today and of tomorrow and of the past? As a human being, you can only face the day as you awake and no more. Just remember His words: "So don't worry about tomorrow; for tomorrow will care for itself. Each day has enough trouble of its own" (Matthew 6:34).

Burden means heaviness. Put down the load of burdens for the past, for today and for tomorrow. Remember the resurrection's power. Remember that

Jesus died and after three days He rose again. He died and paid in full for those burdens. Three days He spent in the grave: past, present and future was paid for. Do not carry those burdens. Put them where they belong: in the future or in the past. Thou shall not steal! What belongs to the future is not for the present and it is not for you either. Catch God's vision. You say, "I don't know how this can be; I don't have the whole picture." Who told you that you need to know, and that you need to have the whole picture? For by faith will He lead you and not by sight. One day at a time you will get the picture. The who, why, when, where, what, and the how are all just details – faith does not need them to bring forth the great miracle. These will come as you move on. If God were to show us all the details about the future, many of us would panic and die of a heart attack. Trust God who said "only believe!" In the midst of uncertainty, behold Him who is Certainty. Gaze upon Him and have a great anticipation of the things to come because you know He gives only that which is good. "Those who hopefully wait for Me will not be put to shame" (Isaiah 49:23).

Is your future like a sealed book? Rejoice, for that is normal. Your life is like a sealed book. The Lamb of God, Jesus Christ who died and rose again, is the only one who can unlock the mystery. To the degree that you let Jesus live in your life, to that degree the mystery will be revealed.

In Revelation 5 we see a book that was sealed. No one, not in heaven, not on earth, and not under the earth, was found worthy to open or read the book and break its seals. But one of the elders announced that the Lion that is from the tribe of Judah, Jesus Christ, has overcome and could open the book and its seven seals.

Not all seals were broken at once. Jesus broke the seals of this book one seal at a time. Little by little the Holy Spirit can reveal to you the things to come, one step at a time. Do not seek to know the future above all things. Seek to know the One who holds the future and you will receive revelation as it is pleasing to the Father. God will lead you by faith not by sight. God loves us; let us expectantly wait for Him.

Allow God to live great and big in you. If He is great in you, everything else becomes small and easy. When persecuted, the enemy wants you to fight this war from the flesh, but the only way you can fight this spiritual warfare is from a spiritual position. The enemy wants you to fight this war from the world, but to win this war you have to fight it from above because God seated us with Him in the heavenly places in Christ Jesus (Ephesians 2:6). Removing yourself from the heavenly position removes you from winning this war. There is not really much you need to do, because this war as far as God is concerned, has already been won. You need to believe in the victory Jesus Christ secured for us, hold on to His word, be strong in the Lord, put on the full armor of God, keeping it on always, and resist the enemy. You need to stand firm, and having done everything to stand firm, stand therefore. Like Stephen who was stoned to death, pray for those who persecute you for they don't know what they are doing!

Against the will of God

There are times you will find yourself in the depth of the sea, under the mighty waters because you have come against the will of God. You might call these trials while you are not putting your flesh to death. It is neither because of the devil, nor your enemies but because you need to submit and obey God. Search your heart and make everything right with God.

Jonah fled from the presence of God. He went against the will of God, Who had said to him: *"Arise, go to Nineveh the great city and cry against it, for their wickedness has come up before Me"* (Jonah 1:2). We see Jonah in the ship to Tarshish. Why is this man on the way to Tarshish when God sent him to Nineveh? Jonah might have a good reason to go to Tarshish, but no matter how he can justify Himself, we all know he disobeyed God. When God requests you to do something, do it immediately, quickly and exactly as He told you. Obey God no matter what the cost. You will be blessed and greatly rewarded. Each pain you go through because you obeyed the will of God will pay great rewards in the end.

Each time the will of man is done rather than the will of God, there will be a stirring up in nature and in all things. The sea will never be calm. If you try to flee to a hiding place, nature itself will revolt against you. Mountains might shake and revolt against your disobedience. The job you try to do against the will of

God will fire you. Money will flee from your pockets since you have refused to use it for God's own glory. Finances and all businesses you undertake will refuse to serve you for you have refused to serve God first. Everyone will know that you are not doing the will of God and no one will be willing to receive you into their ship because everywhere you walk, destruction will follow. They will instead cast you into the sea, into the deep. There you might cry and say *"All your breakers and your waves have rolled over me"* (Psalm 42:7).

As you can tell, that is not a good place to be because you chose it yourself. Men and women of God, learn to be where God sends you and not where you send yourself. God wants you to learn things simply and easily, but if you choose not to, then you will learn them the hard way. In the depth of the water! The currents will engulf you and the breakers and the billows will pass over you.

But remember the mercies of God. Nothing can separate you from the Love of Christ! Nothing at all! Neither height nor depth will be able to separate you from the Love of God. The psalmist knew it so well, he said "He sent from on high, He took me; He drew me out of many waters" (Psalm 18:16). Our heavenly Father's love is beyond comprehension. The mind and knowledge of man cannot understand it. When you call upon the name of the Lord, even in the deep where you go against the will of God, He will come and rescue you. But if you remember to obey and do the will of God, you will save yourself from troubles. Obey the Father. He takes delight in the child that obeys without questioning or running away from His presence.

All things working together for good to them that love God

"And we know that God causes all things to work together for good to those who love God, to those who are called according to His purpose" (Romans 8:28).

What you consider to be hardship is also a grace to you. Don't complain. Always be thankful to God in everything. No matter what adversity you face, always remembering that for the children of God there is but gain. At first when a hardship comes, some people think God has forgotten them. God can never forget His own children. Even though an earthly father might forget his children, God will never forget you. He knows you by name.

In 1997, a few months after I had given my life to Jesus Christ, I woke up one morning and as was my custom, I prayed to my Father. That day, I had to apply for a passport and in order to do so, I needed to obtain some papers which I could only get from the hill country where I was originally from. During that time, this place was still dangerous even after the war. Killings were still being reported in that region and there was no peace. I had no other choice, however, but to go there in order to obtain these important documents. I prayed to God early in the morning asking for His protection and that all would go well, that I would obtain all the documents that I needed. I had a wonderful time of prayer. It was that kind of prayer when you know that God has heard you and has already answered you. God assured me that He would protect me, and that I would be given favor according to His power and perfect will.

I left the capitol city Kigali and went to Rushashi with much boldness and confidence, knowing that God was with me. I did not have my own car so I took a taxi for the 35 mile trip. I obtained all the papers that were needed. Everything went very well except for one thing. When I was ready to come back to Kigali, there was no taxi to take me back! It was getting dark and there was no transport back to the city! I waited and waited, but in vain. As I waited I noticed there was a Daihatsu truck that was used mainly to transport goods. I inquired whether this would be heading to Kigali and whether there was any room for me. I was told that the taxi was about to go to the Kigali city and I then asked the driver for a ride. He denied me a ride, even though he had enough room in the truck.

It was now getting very dark and there was no way to go back to Kigali. I was going to miss work the next day and I just could not understand that! We had many homes during that time in the hill country of Rushashi where I grew up, and seeing there was no car to take me back, I decided to spend the night and started walking towards one of our homes, which was about 4 miles away. As I walked, I reminded God of all that He had told me in the morning that had not come to pass. I said "Oh God how could it be that you did not provide me with transportation back to the city? You know I need to get back to work." It seemed like I was trying to correct God, as if I knew better than Him! I even went beyond and told Him I was mad at Him but God was so silent. He did not say a word!

There I was on my way, walking towards our old home. This was a place of a thousands hills and the only road at the time went across those beautiful hills. I was on the top of one of the hills near the roadside, walking towards home, complaining and nagging against God. Not too long after I started walking, I saw that truck I wanted to get a ride in pass me by. I thought that the driver was so mean, and I kept thinking how unfair he was. As the truck passed by me, I tried to hide my tears, when all of sudden the truck turned below the hill and hit the side of the road or maybe a tree in the corner, and I heard a great noise like that of a bomb exploding.

I did not know what it was first and when I looked I saw that the truck had flipped over and went off the road. The road was across the steep hill, which had other small hills below it and with my very own eyes I looked and saw the car flipping over and over again! It flipped over maybe a dozen times and the back of the truck was full of tons of beer in glass bottles, flipping over and over again. I looked and trembled. I did not know what to do but I remember finding myself on my knees praying to God to forgive me for my self-sympathy and complaining. I asked God to save the souls of the two individuals who were in that truck. There was no 911 there at the time, there was no emergency service, and I did not know what to do. I could see people getting out of their houses to come and help but nobody could do anything. The truck ended up at the bottom of many hills – in the valley. The vehicle was smashed to dust, and there was no hope for life for the two people who had been in the front seat.

Remember, this is the truck I so badly wanted to get on. The truck I thought was the only way to resolve my problem! I stayed on my knees right in the middle of the road, I repented to God and I gave God a chance to speak to me by staying silent. Seeing something like this is a huge wake up call! I indeed listened to what God was speaking to me. Yes, God, you did not get me that ride – you wanted to give me more than a ride! You wanted me to live to proclaim the Gospel. I repented right there for complaining and accusing God for not giving me that ride. Yes, I missed work, and I missed many other things but God spared my life. When I got to the hill country, people gathered together to see me and God used that opportunity for me to read the Bible to old friends and pray for the sick. That evening I shared the gospel with many in that village who came to see me. I was a new Christian. All I knew how to do was to open the Bible and read and tell them all the things I heard the preacher saying. Many in that gathering did not know how to read and they sat there and eagerly listened to the word of life. As I started reading the book of Mark and the miracles of healing, people believed and they were instantly cured. They were amazed about the things written in the gospel.

I could see hope rising within them as I shared this word of life. This was God's plan for me to spend the night in the hill country. This was God's perfect will. If we could only desire the perfect will of God, and if we could only know it, we would never dare do our own will.

To them that love God, all things work together for good. To them that love God, all things can be a way out. No matter what you go through, just remember that there's no loss for the children of God. In the end, there is only gain. The pain, the tears and all the sufferings have no power to kill or harm, but to purify us. At times, many of us don't understand or see any good thing coming through the cross, but if we knew the truth, then we would praise God for the privilege of suffering for His name's sake.

Let me walk in the midst of coals of fire,
Where Your light through me will forever shine.
When darkness arises against me,
I will not be afraid,
But will trust in You,
Because You, O Lord, are resplendent with light;
You have never failed to turn my darkness into light.
The light of Your presence has come
The light of Your presence has risen
against darkness
It will not stop till the whole world is enlightened

Chapter 16: Light Through Fire

From heavenly fire comes heavenly light. The heavenly light will be given only to those fire carriers who act, to those who pass the fire on and who bear fruits. This heavenly light carries life in it (John 1:4). It is a mighty force, a mighty light which casts no shadow; a true light that enlightens every man.

Light awareness

Be full of pure light. *"Then watch out that the light in you is not darkness"* (Luke 11:35). Through you light will shine. Many souls will be won to Christ because of His pure light in you. You will not have to tell people who you are and what you carry inside you. All you have to do is to shine. When a light comes in a dark room, it does not have to introduce itself with words, it does not have to explain or convince people of its reality, it does not have to convince darkness of its power and presence; through acts, light shows its power. Child of God, through your actions make the power of God known everywhere you go. Darkness always recognizes the coming of the light. In the same way, all the people who will come your way will recognize the presence of the light in you. This is the light of God's holy presence and in one way or another, this light must change everyone you meet.

Let your light shine. When people see this light shining through you, they will glorify the Father. People, kings, nations will come to you because of the light of God's presence in you. The light in you will swallow their darkness.

"This is the judgment, that the Light has come into the world, and men loved the darkness rather than the Light, for their deeds were evil" (John 3:19). Those who love the truth will love the light and run towards it. Those who hates the truth will try to run away from the light of God's presence, and they will do so because their deeds are evil. For everyone who does evil hates the light for fear that his deeds will be exposed.

The light of His presence will set prisoners free

Light is not born out of darkness, but darkness dies with the coming of the light. Light will fight with darkness but light always wins. Those who believe in the light are the children of the light (1John 12:36). In the same way that light attacks darkness and always wins, the children of the light must rise up against darkness, attack and they will always win.

With the coming of the light, darkness, horror, and all fear melt away. Where are you stumbling? Which sin is resisting you and which addiction are you not able to let go of? That sin, that addiction is able to hold you because it is hidden in darkness. Bring the light of God into every part of you, every room of your life and let the light shine. The darkness will fade away. It will not resist God's light. Once your whole body is light, sin will not have any hold over you because it won't find any match in you. Light has nothing in common with darkness. God already made a separation between the two "and God separated the light from the darkness" (Genesis 1:4). What fellowship has light with darkness? What relationship has light with darkness but to cast it away? Bring the word of God to that sin, to that addiction, and to that stronghold and you will quickly see how that separation takes place. Allow the light of God to illuminate each room of your life, even the ones marked "private." Truly, the light of God's presence will set the prisoner free.

Walk in the light

Like the fire of God, The light of God's presence differs in intensity. The closer you draw to Jesus, the more light you will receive and radiate. Jesus is the Light of the whole world. Those who draw closer and closer to Him will always bear His light, such a great light. Those who carry the heavenly light will have an overflow of light and it will be passed onto others who come near. In a vision in 1999, I was shown a plain where a great darkness reigned. It was a deep and impenetrable darkness, a deathly darkness! In this plain, many people were playing games of all sorts and they seemed to be accustomed to this darkness for they had lived there too long.

Suddenly, from the sea nearby, there came a frightening violent wave which troubled the water. The water started invading the plain like a mighty flood. Everyone in the plain was seized by panic and they started to run away to save their lives. *"He who walks in the darkness stumbles"* (John 11:7) There was nowhere to run. Dangers met them at every corner they tried to run to. It was too dark and they were running to and from everywhere. I was standing on a mountain called Sinai and in my hand I held a match and a candle that was already lit and had much more candles. The light of my candle was the only light in that place. A great number of those people saw the light I held and they started running towards me. I felt sympathy for these people who had no light and I immediately distributed the candles I had and from one candle that was lit, I passed on the light. Very soon, the whole mountain was lit up with a marvelously dazzling light because of the accumulated light from all of the candles. Many people who were still in the valley were thus saved from the dangers through the light that was on the mountain. Many others, however, had lost their lives there in that valley trying to run away in the darkness.

A man who walks in darkness will stumble. He does not see the way because he does not have the light. Therefore he falls. So it is for the man who rejects Christ, the All-Light. Though he will walk, he will stumble because he cannot see the way. There is no light in him, and if such a man chooses to go his own way, his end is death.

Salted with fire

Fire carriers, light bearers, you who have been salted with fire; you are the salt of the earth! Salt causes people to have thirst. Your words will be like salt to many. This salt will cause those who hear your words to be thirsty for the divine drink. You have power to cause thirst to be birthed even among those who are not interested in the things of God. Fire carriers, light bearers: "you are the light of the world. A city set on a hill cannot be hidden. Nor does anyone light a lamp and put it under a basket, but on the lamp stand, and it gives light to all who are in the house. Let your light shine before men in such a way that they may see your good works, and glorify your father who is in heaven" (Matthew 5:14-16).

Rise up, oh bride of Christ! Attack! Rise up against the darkness. Once you have the heavenly fire and the heavenly light, you will no longer wait to defend yourself from your enemies, but you will attack them. You will pursue your enemies. You will overtake them. You will not turn back until they are all consumed. You are qualified and equipped for this battle. Be full of light. Glow. Only light can fight against the darkness and only the light will be victorious.

The fire is the very flame of the Lord (Songs 8:6). The flame rises up. What can ignite those who are cold? Only the burning flames. The burning heart will be able to ignite the cold and the lukewarm. Only the burning flame can bring the warmth and transmit the fire. Oh, pure flame – rise up, burn divine fire and transmit the fire. Do your task and see the light flowing everywhere.

Praise the Lord. He has made us a light to the nations. Through you and me salvation will reach to the end of the earth. Let righteousness go forth like bright lights. Let salvation go forth like a torch that is burning. Let the righteous shine brightly like the brightness of the expanse of heaven and like the sun and the stars forever and ever. Together, let us set the world aflame, you bearer of heavenly fire and heavenly light, for Jesus our Lord has baptized us with the Holy Spirit and the blazing holy fire.

"I am the Lord; I have called you in righteousness. I will also hold you by the hand and watch over you, and I will appoint you as a covenant to the people as a light to the nations; to open blind eyes, to bring out prisoners from the dungeon, and those who dwell in darkness from the prison" (Isaiah 42:6-7).

ACKNOWELEDGMENTS

*With heartfelt thanks to those who
throughout the journey were helpful*

Apostle Paul Gitwaza: Brother Paul, thank you for preaching the authentic Gospel of Jesus Christ. The Word you preach is truly revealed from the Father, it has revolutionized many people's lives. I always thank God for what He has done in you.

Pastor Sun Warren. Thank you for setting a good example of a true shepherd, thank you for your true love and preaching the message of the Holy Spirit and the fire.

Michael Coleman: Special thanks to my fiancé who stood with me and loves me to the very end. You are very special to me and a friend forever. Honey, I love you and look forward to spending the rest of my life with you serving the Lord!

Deb Lockwood: A special "Thank You" to Deb for the hard and perfect work she did in bringing this book to a reality. Deb spent many hours proofreading and editing this book.

Steve & Rose Hocker: My spiritual parents who set a good example to me and love me dearly. Thank you also for the hard work you did proofreading the Blazing Holy fire.

Sherry Collins: A mighty warrior in the army of God who stood with me in the fire.

Gregg & Catherine Grunenfelder: My host parents who made it possible for me to continue my education in the United States and were used of God to fulfill my many dreams. God bless you abundantly!

Robert Minnick: A brother in Christ who prayerfully and financially supported this work.

Special thanks also to -
David Hocker, Claudine Mujawayesu Leary, Mama Beatrice Ndongala, Emmanuel Glory Ndongala, Steve & Chantal Sundberg, Clarisse Kanziga, Agatha Tibitendwa. Thank you to Pastor Randy Scott of Power Invasion Ministries; Pastor Ray Chavez of New Hope Ministries; Daniel Georgopulos of Hands of The Carpenter. Many thanks to all the prayer warriors throughout the world. Your prayer are accomplishing much – be of good cheer, Jesus is by your side!

**"THANKS" TO YOU ALL! THE TIME IS SHORT. LET US CONTINUE TO SERVE THE LORD IN LOVE.
I LOVE YOU!**

For information, please contact:

The Blazing Holy Fire
Healing Stream Ministries
P O Box 300552
Denver, CO 80203
USA
http://www.healingstream.net
blazingholyfire@healingstream.net

CPSIA information can be obtained at www.ICGtesting.com
Printed in the USA
LVOW06s2304060714

393061LV00007B/49/A